Perfect Phrases for Resumes

Perfect Phrases for Resumes

Michael Betrus

McGraw-Hill

New York Chicago San Francisco Lisbon
London Madrid Mexico City Milan New Delhi
San Juan Seoul Singapore Sydney Toronto

This book is printed on recycled, acid-free paper containing a minimum of 50% recycled, de-inked fiber.

McGraw-Hill books are available at special quantity discounts to use as premiums and sales promotions, or for use in corporate training programs. For more information, please write to the Director of Special Sales, Professional Publishing, McGraw-Hill, Two Penn Plaza, New York, NY 10121-2298. Or contact your local bookstore.

Contents

Contents

Part Three: Perfect Phrases by Industry and Discipline   89

Introduction

Today, resumes are more a part of a job search than ever before. They certainly are more important than they were 10 years ago, when many business experts embraced networking as the key source for finding a new position.

Okay. I do buy into that. Networking is a top source for finding a new position. But even when a candidate is brought to me through a networked source, the first thing I say is, "Have them send me their resume and I will give them a call." Between you and I, after 10 job-search-related books and having managed hundreds of people, it's hard to not be critical of poor resumes. Still, It's table stakes for gaining an interview.

Now, in the e-mail age, all large organizations—and many small ones as well—post jobs on web sites like careerbuilder.com and monster.com, not to mention major newspaper online job boards. What is the first thing you do when you find a job posted you like? You e-mail your resume! You see, in the electronic age of e-mail, resumes play a bigger role than ever before.

I wish you could take the time to sift through a few hundred resumes posted on career web sites and try to find a good candidate. The funny thing is, as difficult as it is for a job seeker, it's

Introduction

pretty darn difficult on the hiring side too. You would be shocked how tough on occasion that's been for me, or my recruiting department, to find good candidates.

I bet as they, and I, have mined through the career web sites looking for candidates, we have passed on many great people. In fact, I would bet the odds are greater than Tiger winning another golf tournament.

Unfortunately, great people still write poor, unflattering resumes. Why?!!! When a hiring manager or recruiter is sifting through resumes, you have all of 10 to 30 seconds to impress them enough to read on. What makes them read on? I'm smiling at the irony as I write this, but it's *perfect phrases*. When candidates write great career summaries and great descriptors of past accomplishments, they get noticed.

That is why I wrote this book. Hopefully, it will help you craft some perfect phrases for your resume.

Perfect Phrases for Resumes

Part One

Resume Basics

On the front page of the employment section of a late 2003 Sunday edition of one of the largest newspapers in the country, there was an article debating the pros and cons of using a resume. One commentary was that the resume is outdated and that in today's world of electronic-based communications it will go away. It went on to say that the resume has long evolved and that the days of using nice stock paper and matching envelopes has passed. At one point it even questioned whether hiring managers want to be bothered with reviewing resumes.

The article was partly correct. The traditional uses of a resume have evolved. Among all the clients we have advised over the last year, none have concerned themselves with paper stock. However, hiring managers and internal and external recruiters do need resumes. What they detest are poorly written resumes that make them work to understand the profile of the candidates.

Resumes are still a huge part of the job search process. The first step in any selection process is to review the resumes of candidates, even those with inside sponsorship. In this section we want to teach you that:

- You need to create an effective and useful career summary for your resume.
- You need to document your accomplishments in the employment history sections and make them line up as closely as possible with the requirements of the company.

People pay hundreds of dollars to have professionals teach them how to present these two things. The career summary, in particular, is crucial. If you were to poll hiring managers, human resources recruiters, and external recruiters, fewer than 10 percent would say they read every bullet describing each job a candidate had. So, if the summary section is weak or nonexistent, there's even less likelihood that the whole resume will be read.

Consider this analogy: Recently I was traveling from Tampa to Dallas. At the Tampa airport I was looking for a couple of magazines to read on the plane. The magazine rack was large and the selection of magazines was broad. I browsed the news periodicals (like *Time*, *Newsweek*, *U.S. News & World Report*), the sports magazines, and some others. I bought two magazines after very casually perusing over 50 magazine covers.

Why did I buy those two magazines out of the whole lot? Their covers and headlines.

In most cases this is not unlike the initial resume screening process for candidates. You can be "deselected" before you ever get to the plate. You need a good resume—a well-presented career summary and employment history documentation—to keep your job search process open and alive with options.

A good resume is no guarantee of obtaining a great position, but a poor one may very well result in your not getting the interview.

Being computer literate is an absolute requirement for any white-collar job today. To be considered a good prospect and a good candidate by hiring managers, good presentation skills can be critical. Hiring managers view the resume and the cover letter as an indication of how well you may perform in the job.

The resume is an indicator of a candidate's:

- Organization skills
- Writing skills
- Presentation skills
- Ability to "net it out" effectively—to communicate clearly in as few words as possible

Your Marketing Brochure

When you see a marketing brochure advertisement, it has been carefully crafted with several things in mind: key messaging, copy positioning, colors, graphics, and so on. Positioning is a critical part of connecting the key message of the advertisement to the instinctive viewing center of the reader.

One more reason the summary is the most important single piece of information in your resume is because of where it rests—right in the visual center of the resume. Imagine an 8 ½ by 11 paper. This is where the visual center of a document is and where your summary should reside:

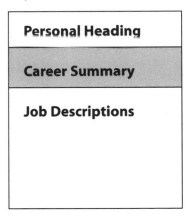

| **Personal Heading** |
| **Career Summary** |
| **Job Descriptions** |

Each discipline or industry of perfect phrases in this book illustrates one or two examples of a career summary you can use in your resume. Feel free to mix and match; with career summaries, you are looking for a crisp format to communicate the most information about you in the fewest words and simplest terms.

Keys to Effective Resume Writing

Have you ever known a highly successful sales professional who didn't have a firm grasp and knowledge of his or her product? Ask any experienced salesperson what the secret to success is and he or she will say that it's knowing the product, knowing the customer, and matching the benefits of the product to the needs of the customer. This is a powerful success formula.

The job search is a sales and marketing endeavor. There is simply no way around this: *You* are the product, *you* are the salesperson, and *you* must define your customers and promote yourself to them. So, like the highly successful salesperson, the key to your success is to know your product (you) inside and out, and match the benefits of the product to the needs of your potential customers (prospective employers). In sales, we call this selling features and benefits.

Regardless of the resume type you choose or the format you decide upon, there are five primary sections that make up a successful resume, along with numerous subsections that can also be incorporated. The five primary sections are:

1. Heading
2. Career summary
3. Employment section
4. Education
5. Miscellaneous sections

Heading

The heading, also referred to as your *personal directory,* consists of your name, address (with full zip code), and phone number (with area code). If you carry a portable phone or pager or have a fax machine, you can include these phone numbers in your heading. We do not recommend that you include a work number. Many hiring managers do not look favorably upon furnishing a work number. They may conclude that if you use your present company's phone and resources to launch a job search campaign on company time, you might do the same while working for them.

Career Summary

Once you read the first three chapters, you'll see why I'm passionate about the value of a strong career summary.

In just a few seconds the reader should get a picture of who you are and what you have done, both functionally and by industry. Here are examples of great summaries:

Career Profile
- Twelve years experience in telecommunications industry.
- Nine years experience in sales and field management, three years in corporate marketing management.
- Created strategy behind wins with many Fortune 500 companies, including Hilton, Norsk-Hydro, National Car Rental, Outback Restaurant, and Harris Corporation.
- Achieved 100 percent plan participation with AEs by developing very creative strategic partnerships that provided alternative, nontraditional sales channels.

Specific Areas of Expertise

- Strategic sales plan development
- Strong financial background
- Establishing sponsorship at account

- Connecting customer needs to corporate solutions
- Understanding customer's business
- Developing alternative selling channels

The reader of a summary like this would need very little time to ascertain the fit of this candidate. The career summary is what gets you noticed and gets the rest of your resume reviewed.

Employment Section

The employment section will have much influence on a prospective employer in determining if you get an interview, and ultimately, a job offer. This section highlights your professional career and emphasizes experience, qualifications, and achievements. The employment module normally begins with your most recent position and works backward (allocate the most space to the most recent positions and less space as you go back in time). Provide the following information for each employer:

1. Name of company or organization

2. City/town and state where you worked

3. Dates of employment

4. Titles or positions held

How It Should Look

When using a chronological or combination format, provide specific information for each employer you worked for and for each job you performed. Include three pieces of information for each employer/job:

1. Basic responsibilities and industry- or company-specific information

2. Special skills required to perform those responsibilities

3. Specific accomplishments

Education

Generally, the education section appears at the beginning of your resume if you have limited work experience. A recent high school, technical school, or college graduate will, in most cases, fall into this category. As your portfolio of experience and achievements gains momentum, the education section will drop toward the end of the resume as newly formed experiences, skills, and accomplishments begin to outweigh educational experience in the eyes of a prospective employer.

You will see examples of how these parts fit together in 10 sample resumes to follow.

Sample Resumes

ROBERTA LYONS

ATHLETIC COACH
Basketball

320 Brandies Street • Springfield, Illinois, 62232 • (618) 555-1212 • email@email.com

9 Years' Successful Experience in High-Visibility Athletic Programs

"Improving Skills—Improving Character—Improving Basketball Programs"

Discipline/Reward/Growth

A positive-thinking, results-oriented, and team-spirited athletic coach with a sound, verifiable record of success in building winning programs and developing values-based students into contributing citizens in their communities.

CORE STRENGTHS

Athletic conditioning and fitness expert

Strategic planning—sound basketball fundamentals

Program marketing and promotions—on/off campus

Nutritional certification

Staff development

Concentration on grades and sport

EMPLOYMENT

Springfield County School System, Springfield, Illinois

Girls Head Basketball Coach/Math Teacher—McKenner High School

1992 to Current

Coaching Highlights:

2001   American Midwest Regional Finals—Top 12 in State

2000   American Midwest Regional Finals—Top 10 in State

1998   Northwest Conference Champions
1997   Northwest Conference Champions
1996   Runner–up Northwest Conference Champions

Coaching Record:

	WINS	LOSSES	PERCENTAGE	COMMENT
2001	15	3	83%	First in conference
2000	14	4	77%	Second in conference
1999	16	2	88%	First in conference
1998	12	6	66%	Third in conference
1997	13	5	72%	Third in conference
1996	13	5	72%	Third in conference
1995	9	9	50%	Sixth in conference
1994	10	8	55%	Fifth in conference
1993	9	9	50%	Sixth in conference
1992	6	12	33%	Last in conference

EDUCATION & TRAINING

Providence College
Rhode Island

Master in Athletic Coaching   1991
Bachelor of Science: Sports Science: Providence College   1988 (Dual)
Bachelor of Arts: Education: Mathematics and Statistics   1988 (Dual)

AFFILIATIONS

National Coaches Federation—Member/Former Board Member, Springfield County Chapter
American Heart Association—Board Member—Springfield County Chapter

References upon Request

deborah lorenz .... data warehouse manager

101 W. 10th Avenue, Denver, CO 80201....e-mail@e-mailaddress.com....303.555.1010

core competencies..

- Data Warehouse Manager offering 10 years of experience and in-depth knowledge of the functional and data needs of e-businesses.

- Data warehouse development experience incorporates skills in programming, analysis, architecture, and project management. Expertise in high-level and detailed system design, requirements gathering, logical and physical data modeling, development, and implementation. Expert knowledge of data modeling in ERP and other major application areas.

- Well-versed in Oracle (Oracle Express, Oracle Reporter, Oracle Financial), Oracle tools, and Erwin products. Data migration experience using Informatica, C++, Java, Corba, multi-dimensional database, JavaScript, Oracle Web server, and Java. Exceptional use of CASE tools as part of an overall development effort.

- Extensive knowledge of DBMS: Oracle RDBMS, SQL, PL/SQL, STAR Schema Modeling. Experienced in UNIX operating system, Microsoft PC operating systems including NT, desktop productivity software, and client/server system architecture.

- Proven ability to assemble and mobilize project teams, building consensus among multidisciplinary technical and functional teams in the rapid development and implementation of data warehousing solutions. Recognized by managers and colleagues as a strong, positive leader and a sharp strategic thinker.

experience..

amazon.com, Denver, CO

Drive the strategic vision and the realization in the evolution from centralized data warehouse, to distributed data marts. Report to divisional IT management with accountability for global processes. Manage a budget of $5.6 million.

- Provide guidance to software development teams on the use and purpose of data warehouses. Direct a team of seven data warehouse developers/analysts in the daily operations of the corporate data warehouse. Oversee all aspects of the warehouses, including data sourcing, data migration, data quality, data warehouse design, and implementation.

- Scope, plan, and prioritize multiple project deliverables, based on data warehousing dependencies and changing business needs. Develop project plans, identify and fill project resource needs, and manage projects to on-time, on-budget completion.

- Influence toolset and business needs assessment. Lead the selection of third-party software; manage vendor relationships. Successfully manage multiple projects in the design and implementation of warehouse functionality and interfaces.

Colorado Department of Revenue, Denver, CO
Data Warehouse Architect, 1990-1996

- Translated an enterprise data model, created dimension and fact tables to support budgeting, financial planning, analysis and data ware systems, in collaboration with the DBA and Data Steward.

- Determined database/data mart business requirements. Created the logical and physical database/data mart design for Relational and OLAP Data Warehouse environment.

education...

Master of Science, Data Warehouse Management, University of Denver, Denver, CO

Bachelor of Science, Computer Information Systems, University of Colorado, Boulder, CO

Melanie Olsen, CRNA

1555 Main Street • Charleston, WV 25302 • (304) 555-8443 • email@email.com

Professional Profile

- **Certified Registered Nurse Anesthetist**
- Bachelor's degree and four years CRNA experience
- Clinical instructor with over 1,000 hours experience
- Outstanding clinical expertise and proficiency
- Attend weekly continuing education meetings
- Excellent problem solver who works well under pressure
- Reputation as a team player with superb people skills
- Upbeat, personable, and highly energetic

Licensure & Professional Affiliations

- Certified Registered Nurse Anesthetist, Certificate #22250
- Registered Professional Nurse, License #0556500
- Member, American Association of Nurse Anesthetists
- Member, West Virginia Association of Nurse Anesthetists
- Professionally involved with local Women's Health Center

"… exhibits high degree of intelligence and readily grasps new concepts … has an affable charm … interacts well with patients, colleagues … even in the most stressful of situations."

James McCroskey, MD
General Anesthesia Services
Charleston, WV

"… reliable and responsible team player … willingly shares the workload … level-headed and competent in an emergency … proficient and knowledgeable in anesthetic skills and techniques."

Barb Schmitt, CRNA
CAMC-Memorial Division

CHARLESTON AREA MEDICAL CENTER MEMORIAL DIVISION
Charleston, West Virginia   1984-Present

☐ **CRNA - Cardiovascular Center** - 1993-Present
Surgeries include arterial bypasses, hearts, amputations, gallbladders, mastectomies, biopsies, major orthopedics

☐ **RN - Medical Surgical** - 1984-1993
RN and charge nurse duties on a 40-bed med/surg unit, included adolescent ward and peritoneal dialysis

Education

- **Certificate of Anesthesia,** Charleston Area Medical Center School of Anesthesia, Charleston, WV, 1989
  ☐ Received Josephine A. Reier Memorial Scholarship Award
- **Associate Degree in Nursing,** University of Charleston School of Health Sciences, Charleston, WV, 1983
  ☐ Received Nursing Student Achievement Award
- **Bachelor of Fine Arts Degree,** *magna cum laude,* Arizona State University, Tempe, Arizona, 1977

"... an excellent anesthetist who remains calm under pressure ... highest integrity ... exhibits excellent leadership ... has been a tremendous asset to our organization."

Lee Ann Smith, CRNA, BA
Instructor, CAMC School of Nurse Anesthesia
Charleston, WV

"... a very responsible employee ... always volunteering for additional assignments ... prompt and punctual ... has a positive attitude ... a valuable asset to our staff."

Tamy L. Smith, Charge CRNA
CAMC-Memorial Division
Charleston, WV

GREG MYERSON

555 Morgan Avenue South ⌂ Richfield, MN 55555 ☎ (612) 555-3106 ✉ gmyerson@email.email

PROPERTY MANAGEMENT PROFESSIONAL

- 10 years of experience managing multiple rental properties, complemented by impeccable credentials.
- Relate warmly to diverse individuals at all levels by using a friendly yet confident communication style.

Asset Management & Valuation	Mixed-Use Property Occupancy	Commercial & Residential
Renovation & Turnkey Operations	Capital Improvement	Site Remediation
Tenant Relations & Retention	Collections	Legal Processes

CREDENTIALS & LEADERSHIP

Certified Property Manager (CPM®)
Certified Commercial Investment Member (CCIM®)
Registered Professional Adjuster (RPA®)
Institute of Real Estate Management (IREM®) Minnesota Chapter 45 Secretary

CAREER CONTRIBUTIONS

- Planned and directed the purchase, development and disposition of real estate on behalf of business and
investors for Minnesota's largest privately owned multifamily housing manager.

down, including vacate notices. Spearheaded and led a marketing campaign, reducing a 25% vacancy to 5% in 4 months.

- Managed receivable activities for 1,600 units. Successfully reduced large outstanding (1-2 months) debt accounts to 25% above acceptable industry levels; maintained these long term.

- Turned the occupancy rate of a 7-building distressed student housing project from 40% to 95% in 3 months.

- Consistently achieved a satisfactory (or better) return on owners' investments.

- Analyzed property management companies' computer needs and implemented updated systems integrating construction and property management software with word processing and spreadsheet applications.

CAREER HISTORY

Property Manager / Marketing Director ▪ HART MANAGEMENT, INC. ▪ St. Paul, MN   1998 – present
34 buildings comprising 440 residential and retail units, plus 346 mini storage units.

Real Estate Asset Manager ▪ STEVEN BYRON PROPERTY MANAGEMENT ▪ Edina, MN   1996 – 1998
Largest privately owned multifamily housing manager in Minnesota.

Property Manager ▪ BLD PROPERTY MANAGEMENT ▪ St. Cloud, MN   1993 – 1996
15 buildings comprising 300+ residential units.

EDUCATION

ST. CLOUD STATE UNIVERSITY – St. Cloud, MN   Degree: 1996

Ariel S. Conroy

email@email.com

212 · 555 · 5555

10 West 25th Street, Apt. B · New York, NY 10001

Event Planning · Public Relations · Media

High-energy, background in fast-paced corporate event planning, promotion, and media relations / production. Possess outstanding cross-industry skills, superior presentation abilities, a passion for excellence, and a contagious enthusiasm. Tenacious and resourceful; will work any hours necessary and will always find a way to get project done on-time / on-budget.

Summary of Qualifications

- Blend creative and administrative abilities to coordinate unique corporate affairs, and media meeting planning for Dun & Bradstreet, Canadian Imperial Bank (CIB), and Jump-Start Productions.

- Manage budgets; select event venues; handle bookings, travel planning, entertainment, and gift selection. Team with design groups to create event ads and collateral materials.

- Function as associate producer on commercials and as media marketer for Jump-Start Productions, a television/cable commercial production firm. Maintain excellent rapport with producers, clients, and high-profile talent.

- Highly experienced in PC word processing, database / spreadsheet design, and presentation development. Familiar with Mac programs.

Areas of Expertise

corporate representation

PR strategies

press releases

presentations

conflict mediation

investor relations

consumer relations

event coordination

budget development

travel planning

meeting planning

Career Highlights

luncheons / dinners
entertainment selection
golf outings
theme design
invitations
corporate gift selection
collateral materials
vendor payment

- Helped plan and deliver Dun & Bradstreet's largest and most luxurious special event, a $1 million golf/spa outing at Pebble Beach, CA, that was attended by nearly three hundred top clients, executives, and their guests.

- Coordinated cocktail receptions, luncheons, company tours, and interviewing rounds for D&B's recruiting events. Created sophisticated spreadsheets to organize hundreds of participants into six $100 thousand events.

- Planned high-profile golf and entertainment excursions and closing dinners for CIIB. Coordinated cocktails, dinner menus and locations, transportation, executive suite at Madonna concert, and other entertainment. Purchased amenity gifts, inspected sites and paid invoices.

Professional Development

PUBLIC RELATIONS AND EVENTS COORDINATOR   1996 to present
Dun & Bradstreet, New York, NY

MEDIA MARKETING REPRESENTATIVE (freelance)   1994 to present
Jump-Start Productions, Inc., New York, NY

SPECIAL EVENTS COORDINATOR / PROJECT ASSISTANT   1991 to 1995
Canadian Imperial Bank, New York, NY

Education

Bachelor of Arts in Communications, Queens College, Flushing, NY, 1990

GRACE MATHERLY

578 Frisco Road ◊ Plano, TX 45237 ◊ H)(214) 555-0254 C (214) 555-3604

Summary

- 10 years experience in professional sales within Fortune 500 arena
- Specialty in high-tech industries, including computer software, telecommunications and consumer electronics
- Specialty within sales is "hunting" – new sales acquisition and relationship development
- Excellent presentation skills, good rapport builder with sales support (internal) and generally self-sufficient

Key Accomplishments

- 2002-2003: Took new sales region with $0 in customer base and in 2 years grew that to over $7MM
- Acquired 2 new "logo" Fortune 100 companies in 2003. Developed the account relationship where no previous existed; designed customized solution for client and closed order within 14 months
- President's Club winner in 2003, 1999 and 1997
- Consistently ranked in top 10% of all sales professionals
- Top salesperson in 1997

AT&T, Denver, Colorado   2001 to Present
Global Account Manager, Mountain Region

- Target Fortune 250 companies in Rocky Mountain region that have no current use with AT&T. Developing customized voice and data solutions for all verticals.
- Won business with third largest corporation in Colorado, representing $4MM in revenue annually for AT&T
- Grew total revenue base of five target accounts from $0 to $7MM in two years.
- President's Club winner in 2003
- Achieved some level of sales penetration in three of five global accounts within 18 months
- 187% of sales plan for 2003; $106% of sales plan in 2002

US West (now Qwest) , Denver, Colorado   1994 to 2001
Sales Representative, Denver

- Representing voice and data solutions for medium size businesses in Denver metro area
- Sales Representative of the Year in 1997
- Specialty was hunting – developing new business where there was previously none.
- Achieved following sales performance:
  o 2000: 163% of sales plan
  o 1999: 112% of sales plan
  o 1998: 210% of sales plan
  o 1997: 230% of sales plan

Patti Coury

555 North 555 Place • Tulsa, Oklahoma 74155 • Residence: 918-555-5555 • Cell: 913-555-5551 • E-mail: pcoury@email.net

Executive Sales

President's Club winning sales professional with 15 years sales experience. Specialty is developing account strategy, sales execution and account management for leading uniform supply company. Verifiable sales performance record with expertise in:

- ☐ Hunting and new account acquisition
- ☐ Account planning
- ☐ Networking with referrals
- ☐ Sales account renewals

Patti is an excellent sales professional. She was aggressive, yet smooth through the sales process. She kept on us, but never turned us off. She developed a solution to meet our needs, and we ended up awarding her 80% of our total share of business for uniform service.

— Emma Thompson, ABC Company

PROFESSIONAL EXPERIENCE

Regional Manager   ARAMARK Industries, Atlanta, Georgia   1988 to Present

Promoted though a series of increasingly more responsible customer support and sales executive positions with the leading uniform supply and management company in the U.S. Currently specialize in custom uniform and apparel design for large multinational firms in Atlanta area. Have been in direct sales since 1995 and have always been ranked in top quarter of country each year.

As a customer service and later sales executive, many challenges have been overcome. This is a vital attribute of a

Situation
- Launched new market segment selling corporate signature apparel to a new and unestablished market with no base from which to grow.

Result
- Developed strict account plan and executed it through first year. Achieved 23% above sales objective in new market place.

Situation
- Increased sales objective in 1999 to reflect need for increased business in response to increased competition.

Result
- With sales quota increase over 35%, continued to meet challenge and exceed quota; ranked number one in sales in 1999

Situation
- Customer churn increased in 2001 due to increased competition.

Result
- Increased customer visits, proactively reviewed contracts, focused on renewals and generally shower more customer interest. Churn decreased in base from 16% in 2000 to 7% in 2001.

Situation
- Promoted to Regional Manager in 2002 while still responsible for revenue acquisition in abbreviated sales territory.

Result
- Exceeded personal sales objective while also achieving as manager: 0 employee turnover, 100% participation in sales plan and maintaining low customer churn.

Situation
- Employee churn and sales rep participation identified as major impediment to successful sales management.

Result
- Selectively hired sales reps and focused on their success through training, account management, team-building activities and employee development. Achieved 0 employee turnover and leading sales performance in SE Region.

EDUCATION   Georgia Tech University, Bachelor of Arts, History   1988

Pete Weldon

50 New England Drive Garden Grove, New York 10576 (516) 555- 7645

NATIONAL ACCOUNTS SALES PROFESSIONAL

Verifiable track record of exceeding sales objectives and winning "logo" national accounts

2003	2002	2001	2000	1999
186 %	132%	240%	148%	155%

Strengths

- Developing strategic plans based on identifying customer functional needs
- Relationship building at the CXO level
- Working effectively internally with support staff
- Exceeding sales objectives and leading sales organization – winning President's Club !

PROFESSIONAL EXPERIENCE

National Accounts Manager, D'ITALIA, INC., New York, New York (1996 to Present)

Senior Account Manager with this $1 billion global clothing manufacturer. Challenged to plan and orchestrate an aggressive market expansion into key leading retailers nationwide. Scope of responsibility includes strategic planning, competitive assessment, market positioning,

- Target Fortune 250 retail companies nationwide to distribute specialty clothing line.
- Won business with second largest retailer in Northeast, representing $4MM in revenue annually
- Grew total revenue base of five target accounts from $0 to $7MM in two years.
- President's Club winner in 2001 and 2003

Retail Manager, SAKINAS, INC. (1988 to 1995)

Recruited to this upscale national retail chain to manage daily operations for start-up and high-growth retail sites throughout the Midwest. Scope of responsibility was diverse and included daily operations management, recruitment, training, scheduling, inventory control, administration and the entire sales, marketing and customer service function. Led a staff of up to 65.

- Led the Chicago store to ranking as the highest-volume operation nationwide.
- Managed the start-up of Detroit store. Recruited 45 personnel, created merchandising displays and coordinated grand opening activities. Built operation to solid first year revenues.

EDUCATION

B.S., Marketing, Syracuse University, New York, 1988

MARIA CRUDO

11935 West 9th Street • Sun Valley, Idaho 83404 • (208) 555-1212 •
email@email.com

SPECIAL EDUCATION TEACHER

Highly dedicated, compassionate, patient, and positive professional with
numerous accomplishments working with the handicapped.

SUMMARY OF QUALIFICATIONS

- Current teaching certificate for Elementary Education—endorsement in Special Education.
- **Quickly develops rapport with students, employees, and staff.**
- Three years' experience (summers) working with handicapped individuals in a Developmental Disabilities Agency and writing programs for handicapped individuals.
- **Manages and promotes self-directed work teams and coordination for three employees.**
- Experienced with licensure surveys for Developmental Disabilities Agencies.
- **Strong leadership, management, and organizational skills; exceptional work ethic.**

EDUCATION

Current Teaching Certificate valid in Idaho and Washington. 2001.

Bachelor of Science Degree in Special Education, Idaho State University, Pocatello, Idaho. 1997.

Developing Capable People Seminar, Temple Elementary, Presented by Stacie Smith. 1997.

Managing People with Handicaps Seminar, Temple Elementary, Presented by Stacie Smith. 1996.

EMPLOYMENT

AIDE. DEVELOPMENT WORKSHOP, INC., Idaho Falls, Idaho. 1994 to 1996.

- Traveled to clients' homes to teach cooking, cleaning, shopping, and budgeting.
- Assisted in writing, developing, and implementing program procedures.
- Taught life skills to clients; ensured the safety of the clients.
- Monitored facility maintenance and security.
- Special project: worked with young boy, age five, who would not speak. After nine months of intense therapy, patience, and special equipment, he began speaking broken words. He is still in therapy and doing very well considering the circumstances.

LAYAWAY/SERVICE DESK CLERK. K MART, Nampa, Idaho. 1991 to 1994 (Part-Time).

CASHIER/COOK. SCOT's DRIVE-IN, Idaho Falls, Idaho. 1988 to 1991 (Part-Time).

Have lived with and cared for a sister and a brother with handicaps.

Tom Anika

123 Arlington Court, Denver, CO 80239
e-mail@e-mailaddress.com
303-555-5451

Summary

- **Voice & Data Communications Engineer** with 10+ years of experience seeking continued project leadership role, integrating emergent technologies into comprehensive communications solutions.

- In-depth knowledge of communications network operations. Proven ability to build proficiency in new technologies and collaborate with multidisciplinary project teams to ensure successful project integration.

- Strong skills in coordinating all facets of multiple complex projects, ensuring on-time, on-budget, on-target results.

- Articulate, flexible, and personable communicator, with excellent skills in client and vendor relations. Frequently selected to serve as a project consultant and task force contributor on critical corporate initiatives.

Experience

Internet Fiber, Inc., Denver, CO   1998-Present
FTTH Project Manager

- Design and build Neighborhood Networks™ (customer-owned Internet Fiber networks) using a high-speed fiber to the home (FTTH) architecture for Internet,

TECHNICAL PROFICIENCIES

Network/Operating Environments:

- Solaris, AIX, Linux, Novell Netware, VMS/CMS Mainframe, DOS, Windows 95/98/NT, Xwindows, Banyan Vines, SunNet Manager

Network Equipment:

- Cisco (1000, 2500, 4000, 7000 series Routers)

- Bay Networks (Contivity 4000 Extranet Switch, BCN and BLN series Routers, 28000, 58000, and 350T series Ethernet Switching Hubs)

- Synoptics (2813, 3000, 3030, and 5000 series hubs/concentrators)

- 3com (3100 series Terminal Servers, Netbuilder II Routers, Lanplex 2500 series, Linkswitch

OneTouch.

Programming / Scripting Languages:

- C, C++, Assembly (370,8086,8031,8051), HTML, FORTRAN, BASIC, Visual Basic, Java, Perl, CGI, SQL, Shell Scripting

Protocols / Services:

- IPsec, PPTP, SNMP, TCP/IP, RADIUS, PAP, MSCHAP, DHCP, DNS, FTP, Telnet, RMON, x.509, DES, Triple-DES, FTTH

Applications:

- Microsoft Outlook, Word, Powerpoint, Excel, Project, Access, Bay Networks Optivity, Harris Network Management, Exceed, Lotus ccMail, Ecoscope, Netscape, Internet Explorer, Visio, Informix, Oracle

---

- Maintain strong partnerships with top-rated residential homebuilders. Coordinate construction schedules from rough electrical to interior finishing phases.

- Hire and manage telecommunications and network technicians and subcontractors to meet all implementation deadlines.

AT&T / Lucent Technologies, Westminster, CO   1990-1998
Telecommunications Engineer, IP-based Network Services

- Supported implementation of multiple projects, including Interspan Network, IP network services (the AT&T Worldnet backbone), frame relay, ATM, AT&T Broadband services, APS (a PC-based, Unix O/S Voice Recognition Call Processing System), and 900 MHz Spectralink phone systems.

- Determined location of hardware and schedule installations to minimize impact to customers.

- Coordinated all unit and system testing, ensuring 100% turn-up of equipment prior to cut-over.

Education

BS, Telecommunications Engineering, Cum Laude
University of Colorado at Boulder

Resume and Job Search Tips

You would be shocked how many typos still exist in resumes today. Sometimes I will review resumes of very experienced professionals and think, "You have got to be kidding me," as I see so many typos. If I were to guide you to avoid typos, it may not mean the same thing to you that it does to me. Here are some specific things to watch that I see all the time:

- Randomly capitalized words in sentences or phrases. If it is not a proper noun or the beginning a sentence, it doesn't get capitalized. You should not use capitalization because you want to add punch.
- Spaces after commas and periods. You need to have them.
- Long, run-on sentences. Look, I am no Stephen King when it comes to creative or effective writing, but I do know short sentences are more powerful than long ones. In long sentences the point gets lost. Tip: If it runs over 1 1/2 lines, it's probably too long. Break it up.
- Use bullets to get your point across. Bullets make it easier to read and get to your point. Is it easier to read *USA Today* or *Don Quixote*?

Internet Tips

- When typing your resume out with the intent of e-mailing it, make sure it is in an ASCII format.

- When you paste your resume in the field provided on careerbuilder.com or monster.com, proof it and reconstruct the bullets and formatting lost, at least with spaces and dashes. Make it easier to read!

- When sending your resume via e-mail in an ASCII format, attach (if you can) a nicely formatted one in case it does go through and the reader would like to see your creativity and preferred layout. If you do attach it, use a common program such as Microsoft Word.

- Before you e-mail your resume, try sending it to yourself and to a friend as a test drive.

- Include your e-mail address on your resume and cover letter.

- Don't e-mail from your current employer's IP network.

- Don't circulate your work e-mail address for job search purposes.

- In the "subject" of your e-mail (just below the "address to" part), put something more creative than "Resume Enclosed." Try, for example: "Resume showing eight years in telecommunications industry" (if that is your chosen industry).

- Be careful of your spelling on the Internet. You will notice more spelling errors in e-mail exchanges than you will ever see in mailed letter exchanges.

Networking Tips

- Remember, networking is a numbers game. Once you have a network of people in place, prioritize the listing so that you have separated top-priority contacts from lower-priority ones.

- Sometimes you may have to pay for advice and information. Paying consultants or professionals or investing in Internet services is part of the job search process today as long as it's legal and ethical.
- Know what you want from your contacts. If you don't know what you want, neither will your network of people. Specific questions will get specific answers.
- Ask for advice, not for a job. You should not contact someone and ask if that person knows of any job openings. The answer will invariably be no, especially at higher levels. You need to ask for things like industry advice and advice on geographic areas. The job insights will follow but will be almost incidental. This positioning will build value for you and make the contact person more comfortable about helping you.
- Watch your attitude and demeanor at all times. Everyone you come in contact with is a potential member of your network. Demonstrate enthusiasm and professionalism at all times.
- Get comfortable on the telephone. Good telephone communication skills are critical.
- Be well-prepared for your conversation, whether in person or over the phone. You should have a script in your mind of how to answer questions, what to ask, and what you're trying to accomplish.
- Flatter the people in your network. It's been said that the only two types of people who can be flattered are men and women. Use tact, courtesy, and flattery.
- If a person in your network cannot personally help, advise, or direct you, ask for referrals.

- Remember, out of sight, out of mind.
- Don't abuse the process. Networking is a two-way street. Be honest and brief and offer your contacts something in return for their time, advice, and information. This can be as simple as a lunch or an offer of your professional services in return for their cooperation.
- Show an interest in your contacts. Cavette Robert, one of the founders of the National Speakers Association, said, "People don't care how much you know until they know how much you care." Show how much you care. It will get you anywhere.
- Send thank-you notes after each networking contact.

Interviewing Tips

- Relax. The employment interview is just a meeting. Although you should not treat this meeting lightly, don't forget that the organization interviewing you is in need of your services as much as, or perhaps more than, you are of theirs.
- Be quiet and poised. Don't talk too much or too fast.
- The key to successful interviewing is building rapport. Most people spend their time preparing for interviews by memorizing canned responses to anticipated questions. Successful interviewers spend most of their time practicing the art of building rapport through the use of powerfully effective communicating techniques.
- Prepare a manila folder that you will bring to the interview. Include the following in the folder:
- Company information (annual reports, sales material, etc.)

- Extra resumes (6 to 12) and your letters of reference
- Fifteen questions you've prepared based on your research and analysis of the company
- A blank legal pad, a pen, and anything else you consider helpful (e.g., college transcripts)
- Dress appropriately. Determine the dress code and meet it. If their dress is business casual, you still need to be dressed business professional. Practice proper grooming and hygiene.
- Before meeting the receptionist, check your appearance. Check your hair, clothing, and general image. Test your smile.
- Secretaries, administrative assistants, and receptionists often have a say in the hiring process. Make a strong first impression on them.
- Your handshake should be firm, made with a wide-open hand, fingers stretched wide apart. Women should feel comfortable offering their hands for firm and friendly handshakes. A power handshake and a great smile will get you off to a great start. Just don't overdo the power handshake.
- Eye contact is one of the most powerful forms of communication. It demonstrates confidence, trust, and power.
- During the interview, lean toward the interviewer. Show enthusiasm and sincere interest.
- Take notes. You may want to refer to them later in the interview. If you are uncomfortable with this, ask permission first.

- Communicate your skills, qualifications, and credentials to the hiring manager. Describe your market value and the benefits you offer. Demonstrate how you will contribute to the bottom line. Show how you can (1) improve sales, (2) reduce costs, (3) improve productivity, and/or (4) solve organizational problems.
- Key in on specific accomplishments. Accomplishments determine hire ability.
- Let the interviewer bring up salary first. The purpose of an interview is to determine whether there is a match. Once that is determined, salary should be negotiated.
- There is no substitute for planning and preparation, practice and rehearsing—absolutely none.
- Practice interviewing techniques by using video technology. A minimum of five hours of video practice, preferably more, guarantees a stellar performance.
- Close the sale. If you find that you want the position, ask for it. Ask directly, "Is there anything that would prevent you from offering me this position now?" or "Do you have any reservations or concerns?" (if you sense that). At the very least, this should flush out any objections and give you the opportunity to turn them into positives.
- Always send a thank-you note within 24 hours of every employment meeting.

Salary Negotiating Tips

- Delay all discussions of salary until there is an offer on the table.
- You are in the strongest negotiating position right after the offer is made.

Resume Basics

- Know your value. You must know how you can contribute to the organization.
- Before going into employment negotiations, you must know the average salary paid for similar positions with other organizations in your geographic area.
- Before going into employment negotiations you must know, as best you can, the salary range that the company you're interviewing with will pay or what former employees were earning.
- Remember, fringes and perks such as vacation time, flex time, health benefits, and pension plans have value. Consider the "total" salary package.
- Listen carefully and pay close attention. Your goals most likely will be different from the goals of the employer. For instance, the firm's main focus might be "base salary." Yours might be "total earning potential." A win-win solution might be to negotiate a lower base salary but a higher commission or bonus structure.
- Anticipate objections and prepare effective answers to them.
- Try to understand the employer's point of view. Then plan a strategy to meet both the employer's concerns and your needs.
- Don't be afraid to negotiate because of fear of losing the offer. Most employers expect you to negotiate as long as you negotiate in a fair and reasonable manner.
- Always negotiate in a way that reflects your personality, character, and work ethic. Remain within your comfort zone.
- Play hardball only if you're willing to walk away from or lose the deal.

- What you lose in the negotiations most likely will never be recouped. Don't be careless in preparing for or conducting the negotiation.
- Be sure to get the offer and final agreement in writing.
- Never link salary to personal needs or problems. Compensation should always be linked to your value.

Part Two

Perfect Phrases by Professional Habit

Introduction

The following phrases may help with your statements. When choosing the phrase that best describes the situation, read it over once or twice in the context of the sentence to be certain that your selection is correct and that the sentence reads well.

Proven track record of/in …
During employment with …, successfully …
Specific responsibilities/functions/duties included …
Total/Complete responsibility for …
Experience involved/included …
Within ___ year/month period, …
In addition to …, responsible for …
Total accountability/Totally accountable for …
Successful in/at …
In order to …, …
Contracted/Subcontracted by … to …
Temporarily assigned to/Temporary assignment(s) included …
___ years' extensive and diverse experience in …
In support of …, …
In support of …, provided …
Specifically concerned with all phases/aspects of …
Expertise and demonstrated skills in …
Due to/Because of/As a result of/By …
Acted/Functioned as …

Sales volume/Profit/Sales quota accountability for …
Extensive and involved academic background in …
By exploiting/using …
… on an individual and group basis/level.
Direct operations accountability involving …
Extensive and diverse practical experience in …
Selected as/Elected to…
… includes the following functional responsibilities …
Reported to/Reported directly to …
… on an ongoing/regular basis.
All of the above resulted in …
Experienced in all facets/phases/aspects of …
Personally responsible for …
… to ensure maximum/optimum/minimum …
Instrumental in …
… included the following management functions …
Direct/Indirect control over …
Provided valuable/invaluable …
Recipient of …
Knowledge of/Experience as/in …
Prior to relocation/promotion …
Constant/Heavy interaction with …
Honored as …
Extensive training in …
In the capacity of/As …
Promoted from … to …
Consistently …
Proficient/Competent at …
Dual/Multiple responsibilities included …
Provided liaison for/between …

Remained as …
Company provides/supplies …
Regularly undertook …
… nationally and predetermined territory.
Won …
Company specializes in …
Concerned directly with …
… from inception to operational profitability.
… ensuring/assuring …
Extensive involvement in …
Served/Operated as …
… from outset/inception to profitable operation.
… allowing/enabling the …
Newly established company/entity engaged in …
Now involved in …
Assigned territory consisting of …
… representing a …
Initially employed to/joined organization to …
Company is one of …
Project(s) involved …
… facilitating a …
Specialized in …
In charge of …
Promoted to …
Innovation resulted in …
Company engaged in …
Familiar with …
Function to …
… amounting to a total savings of …
During association/affiliation with company …

Employed by …

Accountable to …

… saving the company an average of …

Ongoing concern with/responsibility for …

Assigned to …

… for the purpose of …

Recommendations accepted by …

Department/Division consists of/responsible for …

Primarily responsible for/Primary responsibilities included …

… according to …

Cost Reduction

It's no coincidence that the most effective cost-cutters are companies like Wal-Mart or Dell Computer, which use technology to keep processes like inventory management at the cutting edge. Cost reduction in general is a big part of business. It has always had its place, but more since the economic climate softened in 2000. Events since then have compounded the economic stability, and countless companies have taken drastic measures to reduce costs to remain viable. In the telecom industry in particular, cost reduction, not limited to but impacted by workforce reduction, has been paramount for survival.

Here is what you need to be aware of: Cost reduction always has value. You need to position the cost-reduction measures in your discipline to be associated with improved performance of some kind, and not just eliminating a workforce or particular product or function. Associate reduction of costs with improved performance and you'll really have something to talk about.

The phrases below are to be used as a template for a more substantive description of how you drove reduction in costs. You won't be able use all these exact phrases because some are specific to the given candidate's accomplishments. Use them as a guideline to be more specific rather than general. Don't be vague!

Perfect Phrases

- Led team that accomplished a successful turnaround from $1.5 million loss to $.5 million profit in one year; reduced break-even cost by more than 30 percent, and delivered a 50 percent quality improvement.

- Developed and executed corporate development and growth plan for equity investment and refinancing.
- Implemented key operational changes to drive profitability improvements.
- Met or exceeded cost reduction goals by more than 245 percent, delivering over $100,000 in savings in the first year.

Try to be specific so your message does not appear fake or made up. Even this could be more specific.

- Rewrote and implemented new safety handbook, resulting in an immediate 25 percent reduction in worker's compensation claims.
- Reduced costs by redesigning front and back office call center processes for a 100 MM+ annual inbound operation, which led to a cost reduction of 18 percent per member in FY05.
- Developed business case for an inbound telemarketing acquisition vehicle, leading to a significant reduction in acquisition costs (14 percent) and to an incremental 2 million annual registrations.
- Supervised production of printing plant and performed efficiency studies of equipment and operations that resulted in waste reduction from 8 to 3.5 percent, and production increases of 15 percent. Customer complaints reduced to zero.
- Led cost reduction and efficiency activities during revenue downturn, improving bottom line 5 percent, despite 13 percent revenue reduction.
- Implemented cost containment strategies for medical and workmen's compensation programs.
- Chief Negotiator, as well as assisted in negotiations with

UAW and URW. Major achievements in latest UAW contract (6/03) include COLA savings of $1 million and 30 percent reduction in medical absenteeism, saving $2 million.

- Developed and delivered training to employees and customers, increasing knowledge and awareness of quality care and cost containment.
- While balancing the requirements to have a cost effective marketing and distribution system with a progressive organization capable of generating explosive growth, identified cost containment and restructuring opportunities that led to a total 75 basis point decrease in sales acquisition cost, a 32 percent reduction while increasing sales $2.3 billion, almost a 50 percent increase. Cost reductions have allowed for additional promotional opportunities, increased price competitiveness, and a self-financed expansion into new distribution channels.
- Cost of Goods Sold reductions of 7.5 percent while improving customer-perceived quality of finished products.
- Reduced direct labor costs by $2.5 million on annual budget of $12 million. Implemented employee incentive programs, which cost-reduced operation by $1 million.
- Reduction of inventory by $500,000 through sell-back and product rationalization program.
- Accomplished the reduction of inventory by 24 percent, utilizing MRP [Management Resource Planning], JIT [Just In Time], and Value Managed Partnerships with suppliers.
- Directed Corporate Inventory Reduction program, achieving 15 percent reduction in inventories.
- Assigned as Project Manager for the PRI, working with "Global Shared Services," to reduce total cost of ownership ➡

of digital output devices (printers-copiers-faxes), establishing processes, standards, and enabling web access and usage monitoring for cost containment and reduction of nonbusiness activities by minimizing unauthorized use. A 10 to 15 percent cost reduction was projected after a complete cost/benefit analysis and equipment inventory was completed.

- Pharmaceutical Development and Program Management processes ensuring successful implementation and cost reductions of 3 to 5 percent.
- Key member of an executive team responsible for the reduction of over $65 million in annual expenses prior to the purchase of Ameritech by SBC.
- Introduced several procedural and methods changes resulting in a 34 percent cost reduction on a specific product line.

Employee Satisfaction

High employee satisfaction is essential for the acquisition and retention of a quality workforce. Tracking the attitudes and opinions of employees can identify problem areas and solutions related to management and leadership, corporate policy, recruitment, benefits, diversity, training, and professional development. A comprehensive employee satisfaction study can be the key to a more motivated and loyal workforce.

Good managers and good companies realize a happy employee is a productive employee. Poor managers might lead by intimidation, fear, or be too far the other way and appear lackadaisical. A good sports coach knows that to squeeze that extra level of performance, the athlete must be motivated and driven.

Driven and motivated employees will be more creative and work harder to solve problems because they care about their career and about the company or organization for whom they work.

For your part in this, you want to be the manager or employee who creates this drive for excellence, who is able to get the team to perform at a high level by being highly satisfied.

Consider the following phrases for articulating that you have and can create high employee satisfaction.

Perfect Phrases

- Implemented a performance management process that created a strong overachieving team with high employee satisfaction and a less than 5 percent turnover rate.
- Recipient of Award of Excellence in recognition of exceptional employee relations for six consecutive years, as

voted on by management. Exemplifies the important characteristics of high integrity, loyalty, and dedication.

- Focused on building supportive employee relationships with demonstrated responsiveness and confidentiality.
- Resolved employee/employer issues fairly and effectively, which contributed to high employee satisfaction.
- Improved call center productivity at least 40 percent and achieved a high employee satisfaction rating as evidenced by an independent study by planning, managing, and monitoring personnel, labor relations, and training.
- Managed a $1 million project that increased office morale, customer service, and diversity ratings, according to T.D. Finley Rating Survey, by 50 percent.
- Increased productivity 25 percent overall with reduced staff turnover and high employee satisfaction by creating a positive, teamwork environment, setting goals, and sharing the vision.
- Consistently achieved high employee satisfaction, resulting in minimal employee attrition numbers. Maintained a 90 percent or better rate of retention for the senior seasonal staff team, and zero percent turnover for full-time staff for two consecutive years.
- Introduced employee financial/award incentives that improved productivity, reduced absenteeism, and resulted in a 15 percent increase in gross profits. Achieved the highest percentage of employee advancement in the organization. Maintained high employee satisfaction during tough economic times.
- The Southern Region flagship operation was one of the fastest growing and most profitable in the entire

➡

company, and held the highest employee satisfaction rating of all companies in the plastics sector.

- In order to improve employee loyalty and satisfaction, worked with management to create program offering free, in-house leading industry certifications. This program offered employees optional classes in the evenings within our shop for courses leading to certifications such as MCSE and CNE. Visible improvements within employee satisfaction, and had a less than 2 percent turnover during program's two years.
- Provided face-to-face contact needed to resolve sensitive employee issues, including terminations, violence in the workplace issues, harassment/discrimination investigations, and labor relations issues. Partnered with senior/executive business leaders to deploy business initiatives and improve employee satisfaction.
- Responsible for department- and centerwide employee satis-faction results. Achieved improvement in employee satisfaction through implementation of employee-focused initiatives.
- Organized and participated as a lead in task forces set up by management to improve employee satisfaction
- Facilitated employee growth through a culture of openness, continuous feedback, and a practice of prompt decision making (most employee concerns addressed within one working day).
- Lowered employee turnover rate from 35 to 5 percent. Started employee involvement groups to improve morale and safety. Only one recorded injury and no loss time injuries in past year. CEO stated that morale had never been higher.

- Led an organization effectiveness program that improved employee satisfaction by 40 percent in first year.
- Exceeded service delivery goals for quality, quantity, response time, employee and client satisfaction for a 1.2 million member/190-plus employee division; reduced attrition from 50 to 4 percent within one year; directed development of soft skills training program; developed and implemented client relationship management strategies; directed HR activities within the division to improve employee satisfaction and service delivery outcomes; developed and delivered leadership and management training; achieved 120 percent of operational and professional development goals; collaboratively developed divisional budget and delivered all results within budget.

Initiative

The word "initiative" is both a noun and an adjective, and both are valued in business. As an adjective, employees who have initiative are always in demand. Over the long run, they create innovations that create new products, better customer acquisition and retention, and reduce costs.

As a noun, a "business initiative" describes a new innovation, program, or direction. It can be a new sales channel, cost reduction program, or anything new designed to add value. For example, when GE announced an aggressive e-business campaign in 2001, it was designed to increase Internet-based commerce from about 5 to 30 percent. We have new initiatives in business, politics, and sports, everywhere. The important thing for you is to position yourself as someone who may drive or support new initiatives as a means to evolve to remain current and competitive.

Perfect Phrases

- Provided employee training on hazard communication program, ergonomic computer use, and other health and safety initiatives.
- Took initiative to devise a system of referral documents to provide employers with information regarding programs such as respiration protection, hazard communication, and blood-borne pathogen exposure.
- Managed and directed all facets of business development initiatives for Eastern Region; played an integral role in revamping sales philosophies and marketing strategies to successfully lead division to the first profitable year in two years.
- Instituted comprehensive, corporatewide performance

metrics initiative with the slogan, "You can't manage what you can't measure," resulting in a proactive—instead of reactive— management of the company.

- Developed and managed sourcing strategies for high volume initiative to include virtual job fairs, proactive research, and an on-site job fairs in multiple locations.
- Primary responsibility is for worldwide field engagement, specifically, aligning Account Managers with Client Business Managers in AT&T's most strategic accounts.
- Developed and implemented a Proactive Teaming Initiative with sponsorship from both sales and marketing. This initiative required active facilitation of joint account planning meetings between the Account Managers and the Client Business Managers to identify pockets of opportunity in those accounts in which both sides would benefit. Also responsible for developing additional incentive and promotional programs that lifted sales results 23 percent over previous year.
- Collaborated with Finance to reduce Accounts Receivables collection cycle by implementing a proactive discrepancy resolution initiative. Revised procedure increased available cash by $1MM annually.
- Developed proactive marketing initiative to maintain company's leverage and protect future interests while meeting market expectations for standardization and integration.

Listening Skills

Many people say they are good listeners. In fact, I've never met a candidate who said he or she was a poor listener. No one ever writes "poor listening skills" on their resume. Some should, if they were honest or knew themselves! However, so many are in fact weak in listening skills. I can recall many interviews where I've asked questions and gotten a response that is a 50 percent hit and the rest is babble that clutters the original point and renders them too wordy. You've heard that silence is golden? The interview is where you demonstrate just how good your listening skills may be.

The resume is where you may try to describe in writing that you do in fact have good listening skills. Generally speaking, I am not a fan of even using "good listening skills" on your resume or attempting to go in that direction. It's too vague, too hard to validate.

Consider these phrases if you must use this trait; for example, if you are in sales, social work, or health care, where listening skills are vital to success.

Perfect Phrases

- Possess strong analytical and assessment skills. Keen listening and negotiating abilities facilitate understanding of all facets in decision-making process; this results in reputation for writing solid packages and good business for all parties. Proven ability to cultivate new accounts, establish strong business relationships, and immediately contribute to operations.
- Led resolution of employee inquiries concerning policies, procedures, programs, or personal problems through active listening and standard coaching methods.

➡

- Good empathetic and listening skills; ability to use knowledge to systematically solve problems. Facilitation and team development skills; strong interpersonal and influencing skills.
- Exercised listening skills and patience toward adolescents and adults struggling with substance abuse. Empathetic listening is a critical part of social work to gain trust and belief in working toward improvement in behavior.
- Furthered corporate identity and sales with effective presentations, established rapport based on well-developed listening skills and ability to match desires with product. Profitably directed key account management and distributor management programs. Was recognized every year for outstanding distributor development. Increased direct sales by 100 percent and increased distributor sales 135 percent during nationally difficult economic times.
- Fostered consultative relationships with customers to attain 20 percent annual increase in new business production. Skills exercised included leading, listening to customer needs, connecting solutions to those needs, and effective follow-through.
- Presented parenting skills workshops emphasizing play and motor skills, active listening, problem solving, behavior modification, positive self-image, and single parenting.
- Excellent listening skills, and ability to pay particular attention to detail. Was able to consistently uncover new sales opportunities by keying in on client trends, where other sales managers might have overlooked them. Able to listen and respond to all functions within an organization, from Finance to Sales and Marketing to Production.

Managing Conflict

Certain types of conflict—over a new product idea, for example—are potentially creative and can be enormously beneficial to the organization. This sort of conflict should be encouraged, although it may still need handling with care.

When conflict becomes personal, however, it is often negative and destructive. This type of conflict may arise from a range of causes. They can include poor communication, misunderstanding, problematic working conditions, unrealistic work expectations, discriminatory behavior, skill deficits, lack of resources, selfishness, stress, or depression. This destructive form of conflict can also result from a difference in personal opinion, the causes of which may lie outside work altogether.

You need to position yourself as one who manages conflict well, that you grow teams, keep morale high, and drive your team or projects to "strive, stretch, and reach."

Perfect Phrases

- Resolved conflicts between departments to ensure personnel were available for flights, conducted team leader meetings, and resolved all customer problems.
- Developed and led Conflict Resolution program in K-6 schools, linking leadership program with life skills awareness within a Baldrige in Education framework.
- Acted as liaison between executives, tenants, brokers, and corporation, managing conflict and ensuring shared understanding, accountable for coordination of final agreements.
- Responsible for driving change and managing new staffing model utilizing "workout" change model by leading a team of 30 cross-functional managers.

➡

- Reviewed annual culture survey results and consulted with management teams on potential suggestions to enhance/improve culture.
- Facilitated several conflict resolution sessions between operations and functional groups.
- Facilitated new manager assimilation sessions.
- Facilitated change management workout sessions.
- Demonstrates strengths in managing diverse job processes, building and maintaining relationships throughout an organization, motivating staff and colleagues, assessing and developing high potential talent, and managing corporate objectives through major change.
- Managing Conflict—AT&T School of Business, Course MS6431, completed.
- Managing People and Performance—AT&T School of Business, Course MD7601, completed October 1993.
- Certifications: Numerous technical and managerial courses: Managing People and Performance, Managing Conflict, Communications Workshop, Leadership for the Future, Achieving Communication Effectiveness, and Labor Relations (AT&T School of Business & Technology).
- Contracted Trainer for specialized workshop programs.
- Programs topics include: Stress Management, Interpersonal Communication Skills, Career Management, Customer Service Skills, Conflict Resolution, Understanding and Managing Change, "Who Moved My Cheese?" Team Building, and Assertiveness and Self-Esteem.
- Prepared training materials and instructed workshops on Stress Management, Understanding and Managing Change (incorporating "Who Moved My Cheese?" materials), Career Development and Advancement.

➡

- Selected local facilitator for the nationwide training broadcasts Coaching Skills for Managers, Planning and Organizing, Oral Communications and Listening Skills, Training Aids, and Training Technology Update.
- Certified facilitator for group feedback sessions for managerial and support staff that completed the training assessment instrument for the "Performance Development System."
- Contracted Instructor for school's two- and three-day training courses.
- Programs include: Conflict Across Cultures, Assertiveness Skills, Constructive Conflict Resolution, Negotiating Techniques, Dealing with Workplace Negativity, Effective Customer Service, Interpersonal Communication, and Creative Problem Solving.

Oral Presentation Skills

Oral communication skills are critical to the success of individuals and their organizations. This is equally true whether you are communicating one-to-one, or one-to-250. A good presentation has the power to deliver your message and the emotional force to move your audience to new ways of thinking and/or behaving.

Delivering oral presentations or having excellent oral presentation skills is important to any position, but perhaps more vital to those in training, sales, marketing, consulting, and in senior management positions in general. In almost every resume I read the candidate writes "excellent oral [or presentation] skills." Okay. So what? Everything you write should answer the question: "So what?"

Consider modeling your phrases the way the following, which are more specific, are written.

Perfect Phrases

- Excellent oral skills: presentations that excite and inform, speeches—prepared and extemporaneous. Training skills include developing and delivering training curriculum, including the presentations and workbooks.
- Presentations: engaging speaker and seminar leader, sales presenter, and technical management liaison. Enjoys a natural ability to work with others, influence C-level decision making, and promote company products and services to a wide range of targeted prospects, alliance partners, and vendor leaders. Create and present executive-level seminars and workshops, create goodwill and future interest at corporate trade shows, and author specialized articles and procedural documentation. Establish quick ➡

rapport with coworkers, professionals. and staff. Exercise diplomacy and tact; enjoy a reputation of excellence in relationships.

■ Promote company products through oral presentations in a variety of venues, including trade shows and conferences to create exciting buzz. Regularly requested to speak at industry trade conferences [you might be specific here] and global billing and trade shows.

■ Communicate compliance results to corporate management through oral presentations and written reports.

■ Conduct corporate staff presentations and creative employee training seminars.

■ Responsible for new product presentations and sales techniques throughout California.

■ Gave over a thousand lectures, primarily for Ford Motor Company, Fidelity, and Anderson Consulting. Recognized by *Marketing and Sales* magazine as one of the top 10 speakers in the United States. Recognized by the WTC in Dallas as "America's number one motivational technology speaker." Featured in many magazines, and has written three books published by McGraw-Hill.

■ Wrote keynote speech for a motivational speaker. Doubled the original content through extensive research and interview. Made countless revisions to make the tone and texture of the language sound consistent with the speaker's personal style. Received excellent audience feedback and a repeat invitation to be the speaker.

■ Motivational speaker (current): as a speaker, contract out with various organizations to bring exciting and educational presentations to schools and businesses.

Speak to audiences that range from 100 to 2,500 people. Speak to an average of 15,000 people a year.

- Marketing/motivational speaker: participated in training classes through the delivery of entertaining and informative lectures to middle and high school students. Topics include those that encourage and support self-confidence, social skills, etc. Audience number ranges from 30 to somewhat more than 300.

- Prepare and deliver exciting and informative lectures/workshops on a variety of topics, with emphasis on positive thinking and personal empowerment. Some topics of discussion include interviewing techniques, clarifying goals, personal life mission statement, believing in yourself, and living your full potential.

- Communication: communicate well when speaking and writing; excellent public speaker; conducted training seminars for candidates, volunteers, and party activists; able to act as a liaison between different personality types; comfortable and effective communicating with both superiors and staff.

- Leadership: able to motivate a project team; background provides wide range of interpersonal skills to encourage and lead others.

- Management: known for a contagious passion for excellence, a talent for resourceful business solutions and motivational leadership. Effectively use an empowering, participatory management style that encourages accountability, teamwork, and the continuous improvement of desired results.

- Team building: in business, organizational leadership, training and education, recognized for ability to merge

dissimilar people into cohesive teams with common focus.
- Communication: challenging motivational speaker. Excellent communication skills; experienced in motivating and inspiring both large and small groups of individuals in common vision and purpose. Extensive presentation skills.

Organizational Skills

I interviewed a candidate named Steve some time ago and hired him based on his ability to manage multiple projects simultaneously. His resume said: "Excellent organizational skills." Then I worked with him, and within 90 days it proved to not only be untrue, but just the opposite. Steve could not plan or manage multiple projects or issues simultaneously. Sometimes I wondered how I missed it in the interview. I was faked out. I now discount that phrase "excellent organizational skills" as a hiring manager unless it is supported.

That's the key: to support the skill with some backup so it seems credible and not resume fluff. Consider the phrases and how they are supported. Notice that the actual phrase "organizational skills" is not always present; it is implied, and therefore perhaps more powerful.

Perfect Phrases

- Achieves win-win outcomes; strong communication and organizational skills with an acute attention to detail; ability to manage multiple projects; efficient, organized, detail-oriented, self-starter' good analytical, follow-through, and decision-making skills.
- Consistently bringing projects to a successful finish on time, on budget.
- Successfully managing multiple projects simultaneously, using effective time and priority management skills.
- Promoted to lead the Project Management Team. Responsibilities included managing all aspects of the division's business and systems projects by preparing and managing project plans, scheduling, and facilitating status meetings; also, evaluating and analyzing cost-

➡

benefit relationships, documenting, and communicating issues

- Responsible for marketing, coordinating, and managing vendor services for large corporate accounts. Represented multiple regional vendor services specializing in worker's compensation, auto, medical malpractice, and disability insurance. which required excellent organizational skills and project planning.

- Brought on to provide risk, logistics, inventory, facility, and warehouse operations management, including personnel supervision for a leading remanufacturer of consumer electronic products. Possess excellent organizational skills required to manage all functional areas properly. Responsibilities included coordinating international logistics between multiple manufacturing and refurbishment centers, and establishing and managing the reverse logistics department, handling over 15,000 units per year.

- Efficient in managing multiple projects simultaneously while utilizing excellent organizational/critical thinking skills and good judgment; consistently able to provide high-level, systematic standards of performance.

- Fifteen years experience in managing multiple projects simultaneously, including the ability to work under pressure, meet tight deadlines, and utilize problem-solving skills to ensure projects met stated goals and objectives.

- Highly successful project manager of lead and revenue generation programs, with particular skill in managing multiple projects simultaneously from concept to completion.

- Partner Program support: managed the production and distribution of Electronic Partner Packages, multiple collateral projects (data sheets and Division Overview brochure), trade show collateral, and signage requirements

- Effectively managed integrated marketing programs on limited resources from development and implementation to program reporting and analysis.

- Experienced at consulting with teams, to understand their needs, uncover opportunities, and recommend creative ideas and solutions.

- Proven skills in organizing, prioritizing, and managing multiple projects simultaneously on time and budget. Effective working independently or leading a team with minimal direction toward broadly defined objectives.

- Interfaced with three regional sales centers and field marketing to develop projects targeting installed customers to increase customer loyalty. Developed and managed integrated marcom projects from concept to completion.

- Managed the creative development of sales literature, including product software specification sheets, brochures, reference guides, and case studies. Ensured completion of projects on time and within budget guidelines. Worked with various agencies regarding copywriting, design, and print production, managing multiple projects simultaneously.

- Recruited for coordinating, analyzing, and developing a communication strategy to ensure that group goals were being tracked and met project deadlines. Developed streamlined project tracking processes, which resulted in acquisitions of over $53 million, while managing multiple projects simultaneously with outside vendors.

- Increased production efficiency by managing multiple projects simultaneously, including client relations, schedules, and deadlines.

➡

- Adept in designing brochures, collateral, annual reports, and flyers, as well as conference, exhibit, and presentation materials, advertising, campaign materials, web sites, and many other design projects.
- Expert at Project Management and CRM Direct Mail projects using in-house databases. Experienced in all areas of targeted marketing, retail management, and ad production and printing, and at managing multiple projects simultaneously.
- Developed a strategic marketing plan for the company, researched and evaluated new safety software, provided detailed case research and accident reconstruction support for ongoing litigation, and published press releases.
- Managed multiple projects simultaneously in a consulting firm atmosphere; broadened background and enhanced skills and knowledge in the field of safety through design.

Problem Solving

A manager's primary function is to solve problems. Understanding his or her own approach to problems and the problem-solving style most often used is an essential early step to becoming a more effective creative problem solver.

Managers tend to deal with problems in one of three ways:

1. Avoid them—refuse to recognize that a problem exists. Not quite the strongest managers, but I have had the pleasure of knowing some of these folks. Some people just don't understand that most problems do not self-correct.
2. Solve them as necessary—deal with the urgent. Better, but still not senior management material.
3. Seek them out—anticipate, to avoid them becoming urgent. Ah, here you go. This is where you need to position yourself and represent your skills on your resume and on the interview.

Articulate in your resume and interview that you are the latter.

Perfect Phrases

- Recognized abilities in problem solving, with a strong background in Methods and Time Studies for setting Production Standards. Managed the startup of a new state-of-art distribution center. Particularly effective in assessing and resolving employee conflicts and organizational problems, allowing for increased productivity.
- Developed strategic relationships with various department heads and suppliers, which significantly facilitated

communication and problem resolution capabilities within the organization.

■ Implemented the following structured programs and methods into the engineering department: Advanced Quality Planning, Dimensional Control Plan Plus, Failure Mode and Effects Analysis, Design of Experiments, Quality Operating System, 8-D Problem Solving, Continuous Improvement Plan, process potential studies, preventative maintenance, packaging engineering, flow charts.

■ Applied strong interpersonal and communication capabilities in working with a wide range of personnel at all levels to gain valuable insight, avoid potential problems, and facilitate the timely completion of projects.

■ Successfully implemented customer deductions program for Claims Department, which identified problem areas within the corporation and reported results; made recommendations to upper management on a daily basis.

■ Veteran production manager experienced with quality assurance, problem solving, streamlining processes, and optimizing production work flow. Extensive experience in project management, creating intuitive business collateral, Internet promotion, and developing proactive marketing strategies. Creative experience in the following:

Strengths in problem-solving ability, analyzing the symptoms, identifying what is wrong, and finding the solution. Also, strong in conceptual intellect.

Creative problem solver. Ability to move beyond limiting questions and to nurture problem-solving ideas through each of four phases of creative problem solving.

Strategic thinker, 10 years solving design, communication, and process problems.

Management/problem solving/communication skills: managed all print and presentation projects with over a 95 percent on-time rate. Handled project tracking, system/file management, estimating, budget/billing, vendor billing, and liaisons with all vendors.

- Administration, Planning, and Problem Solving:

    Oversee multiple tasks with varying priorities, work with many departments within an organization to ensure smooth operation, productivity, and marketing; identify areas of improvement; research, develop, and implement improved procedures.

Reengineering

The only thing that doesn't change is "change" itself. In a world increasingly driven by the three Cs—Customer, Competition, and Change—companies are on the lookout for new solutions for their business problems. Recent headlines in the mainstream press that reflect these changes include, "Wal-Mart reduces restocking time from six weeks to thirty-six hours," and, " Hewlett Packard's assembly time for server computers touches new low—four minutes," and, "Taco Bell's sales soar from $500 million to $3 billion." The reason behind these success stories is reengineering.

Reengineering is the fundamental rethinking and radical redesign of business processes to achieve improvements in measures of performance such as cost, quality, service, and speed." Since the softening of the economy in 2000, reengineering has redesigned many corporations. In the late 1990s AT&T was a powerful force in telecommunications. In 2005, AT&T has exited its consumer business and is a mere shadow of its former self.

Reengineering is not always a reduction in the size of the workforce. The workforce reduction that may accompany can instead be a by-product of a company changing itself.

In terms of your resume and interview, you should think about noting whatever experience you've had in affecting these reengineering changes in the past.

Perfect Phrases

- Initiated turnaround with a complete restaffing of entire marketing organization. Recruited qualified personnel, introduced internal training programs, redesigned core processes, enhanced technologies, and created a sophisticated and responsive organization. Provided executive team and senior operating management with meaningful financial data.

- Redesigned organizational structures and business plans for the corporation. Introduced series of personnel and executive incentive plans that enhanced performance and accountability.

- Relocated corporate offices, field organization structure, and associated equipment for 9,300 employees in less than 120 days.

- Facilitated several successful turnarounds, introduced standardized financial and accounting processes, upgraded technologies that improved financial condition from flat line growth to net income increases from 2 percent first year to 14 percent in year three, highest in industry.

- Expert in the use of Business Process Reengineering to optimize work flows prior to developing or introducing new technology.

- Directed national cost study and methods reengineering program that achieved more than 10 percent savings per review.

- Senior Lead Management Consultant to Citibank's Business Division, directing work in reengineering design, development, testing, business analysis, and implementation of Citibank's enterprise migration and conversion. Provided senior management direction in gap analysis, data architectural design and functionality, vendor relationship decisions and implementation guidance.

- Process reengineering, commercial markets:

    Responsible for building an infrastructure to support new marketing initiatives, integrating traditional long distance into bundled offerings for the prospect segment directorate.

Led a major reengineering project to automate the marketing program release processes, including an intranet marketing program offer and message template generation system, an automated data feed to all downstream processes, and a redesigned database algorithm to optimize table size and vendor performance. This project dramatically reduced marketing program cycle time and recycle errors.

- Specific areas of expertise include Risk Management, Operations, Manufacturing, Project Management, Product Management, ERP, Business Process Reengineering, Change Management, Client and Customer Value Management, as well as the integration, customization, and implementation of Distribution, Supply Chain Management, Purchasing, AP, AR, GL, Billing, PeopleSoft, and SAP applications for small to large corporations.
- Served as the team lead for the redesign of member customer service processes for a major state health maintenance organization (HMO). Led the creation of conceptual design models, business procedures and rules, decision trees, and templates to support customer service process and tool implementation.
- Facilitated an organizationwide reengineering effort to reduce costs, improve efficiency, and increase resources. Established and enhanced relationships with vendors, partners, and subcontracting companies to ensure on-time implementation of systems.
- Credited with reengineering IT operations and establishing new enterprise computing environment within nine months.

- Created and implemented IT processes, procedures, and standards:

  > Planned and designed network and topology architecture. Directed teams in reengineering network infrastructures and migrating company from Token Ring to Ethernet topology. Managed the implementation of WAN to ensure appropriate data access and integration throughout all locations, including firewall and security strategies.

- Promoted renewed commitment across the IT division to change management process and practices, doubling the level of regular participation in weekly change management meetings, greatly improving interdepartmental coordination with regard to middle to high visibility changes.
- Refocused, realigned, and sized sales force territories based upon detailed customer segmentation, opportunity fit analysis, and change management.
- Developed a process for production test, implementation, and change management, as well as security policy, systems performance process and reporting, migration process, and redundant facilities environments.
- Responsible for the quality of service delivery to multiple business units and trading operations, project management, problem escalation, crisis management, change management, and service level standards across multiple platforms and network systems. Key member of change management panel.
- Evaluated help desk functions, focusing on structure and strategy, perception and performance, methodologies and procedures, staffing and education, systems, and ➡

technology and management reporting. Managed all change management initiatives to improve these functions.

- Consulted with customers and managed multiple projects such as information security and access control, enterprise change management, disaster recovery and business continuity planning, and new core network build-out support.
- Engaged in the instructional design, courseware development, and deployment of end user training. Developed business process procedures, functional scripts, and change management deliverables.
- Directed a cross-functional team to custom-build an intranet-based application that enabled time management, team collaboration, and project management. Integrated the solution with Hyperion and PeopleSoft and facilitated a nationwide rollout of the application.

Time Management

Time management is a giant skill for a successful person, in any discipline. No question. So many people think they have it, and so few do. I had a vice president several years ago who used to say, "Give me someone smart, passionate, and who knows how to use their time, and we can give them the experience." Same with time management for me. It's vital to success. If you can convey that you effectively manage multiple projects simultaneously, you will be much more valuable to your prospective employer. Then call me because I want you working with me!

Don't let anyone steal your time. It is priceless and should be guarded with care. Benjamin Franklin once said, "Dost thou love life? Then do not squander time, for that is the stuff life is made of." More recently, former Secretary of State Henry Kissinger said, "There cannot be a crisis next week. My schedule is already full." Needless to say, the most valuable commodity in the world is time. It is easily wasted and can never be replaced; therefore, time management is essential.

Consider the following phrases candidates might use to convince employers that they use their time effectively.

Perfect Phrases

- Expertise in finding out how much time is worth, concentrating on the right things, deciding work priorities, planning to solve a problem, tackling the right tasks first through prioritized "to do" lists, and executing the plan in a timely fashion.
- Extensive project coordination, prioritization, and details/time management techniques.
- Employed outstanding time management and resource

allocation skills to coordinate multiple tasks while maintaining strong quality focus.

- Organized, detail-oriented, and self-motivated, with excellent time management, prioritization, and multiple task/project coordination skills. Strong work ethic and professional attitude emphasizing reliability, integrity, teamwork, and the willingness to work as necessary to get the job done.
- Certified in Time Management, Franklin Time Management course.
- Proven ability to prioritize tasks, organize and coordinate activities, manage time, set and achieve goals, meet deadlines, develop relationships, and establish procedures.
- Sponsor of 80:20 program at Toyota, which argues that typically 80 percent of unfocused effort generates only 20 percent of results. The remaining 80 percent of results are achieved with only 20 percent of the effort. Led initiative to improve time management skills of 670-plus employees.
- Assisted the production coordinator by leading the floor, training the staff, and pulling statistics. Skills used: Time Management, ability to meet strict deadlines, and ability to work under pressure.
- Business Analyst MPS/FI Project SAP Time Management:

  Assisted in the implementation of SAP R/3 as the time management deployment lead. Directed the implementation of the time management module at each mill site. Lead the site payroll and HR personnel with data mapping and conversion. Instructed site power users and end users in time management training classes.

➡

- Effective use of time management, understanding the key principles of time management to become more effective and efficient. The essence of time management can be expressed in five major points:

  > Know the big picture.

  > Understand the difference between urgent and important.

  > Learn to think and act in a proactive way.

  > Use weekly planning as your major tool.

  > Avoid time wasters.

- Employed outstanding time management and resource allocation skills to coordinate multiple tasks while maintaining strong quality focus.
- Certifications: Active Listening Course; Decker Communication Course; Franklin Time Management.
- Time Management: able to manage multiple assignments and maintain quality of service under fast-paced conditions.
- Two full life cycle implementation of Payroll with ADP, time management, and organizational management, personnel administration. Attention to detail and ability to prioritize multi-upgrades activities along with excellent communication skills. Experience with working in a team-oriented environment, and an outstanding problem solver.
- Time Management: work schedules and time recording—substitutions, absences, absence counting, absence quotas, leave entitlement, FMLA (Family Medical Leave Act) workbench, overtime, availability—as well as and time evaluation.

➡

- Involved in training the clients' project team and determining global template functionality for the global project team in the USA. Duties included project plan preparation, progress reporting, training of local project team, determining local requirements, identification and specification of system interfaces, final configuration of the system, system and acceptance testing. Modules configured and implemented were PA, PD, Training and Events, Recruitment, and Time Management.
- Project planning experience to list out tasks, prioritize them, and map out execution. Does not procrastinate, uses time wisely, plans exceptionally, employs use of Covey planning system.
- Provide relevant and timely sales and time management training:

  Conducted training needs assessments to determine training shortfalls and needs.

  Attended several sales and time management courses (i.e., Covey, Franklin, Career Path), developed and conducted specific training courses that addressed the needs of the business.

  Provided consultation services in time management training to two corporations.

Written Skills

Having written a dozen books on topics like the one in this book, I am biased about the importance of writing in business. I majored in accounting and never thought about writing early in my career. In fact, pride had more to do with my attention to detail in writing than anything: I never wanted to be caught with a typo or incorrect grammar and have the reader think I was less professional or not queued to be promoted.

Then e-mail entered the workforce in the mid-'90s and poor writing skills were exposed more than Pete Sampras's fast court game on red clay. Sometimes my managers get irritated because I will take the time to rewrite poorly written e-mails or those with typos. I bet some even snicker behind my back, and were I not published, it would be even worse. But not most of my colleagues—only the ones who are lazy and lack the drive to excel.

Still, good writing skills are an absolute reflection on your professional skills. Much of it is in proofreading and some attention to detail. I'll tell you this: When you write poorly, people think less of you professionally.

Demonstrating excellent writing skills begins with your resume. Here are some phrases to consider in order to validate that you do in fact have excellent writing skills. Note how detailed and specific some of the descriptions are. As a hiring manager, I would not doubt the writing skills of candidates like these.

Perfect Phrases

■ Wrote preview briefs for two clients for the upcoming CES Show in January 2005.

➡

- Built briefing books for clients utilizing information obtained from various sources.
- Took the initiative to sort out the magazine lists and ed cal lists—giving them the chance to refocus their top tier, thus giving their clients a better service level.
- Validation of other consultants' plans, thoughts, and presentations for their clients.
- Provides consulting, business plan, and market plan assistance; prepared multiple presentations, marketing brochures, and mailing programs for a diversity of companies.
- Worked with Creative Directors, training manager(s) to develop, implement, create, and design staff instruction manuals, newsletters, web pages, policy and procedure manuals, and announcements to publicize various training programs using Excel, PowerPoint, Word, and Lotus Notes.
- Assisted in layout design and production of printed materials, including newsletters, brochures, slides, graphs, and other visual PowerPoint presentation materials. Created Excel/Access spreadsheets, database, word processing, and graphics computer software programs. Conceptualized and designed layouts and formats for brochures, annual reports, direct mail, newsletters, advertisements, and corporate imaging.
- Highly resourceful, possesses strong merchandising and visual presentation skills. Strong attention to detail and keen sense of color, balance, and scale. Ability to expand on creative ideas and concepts.
- Additional duties include:

    Proposal writing

    Presentations

➡

Technology auditing

Contract writing (including Statement of Work)

- Client communications, product branding, product rollouts (creative and tactical implementation), communication templates, proposal style guides, process documentation, ad campaign development.
- Collateral development: writes copy for marketing pieces, including but not limited to product sheets, press releases, brochures and flyers, ad copy, board reports, client communications.
- Proposal writing for various business lines, effective content with high-impact responses, high-quality proposal packaging, strategic messaging and targeting.
- Media and public relations: development of strategies to heighten awareness and visibility in the industry, speech-writing, media collateral, and kits.
- Online communications/web writing: concept and copywriting for web site and multimedia demos.
- Web design using HTML, Basic Management program, and several advanced writing and communications courses including Effective Writing for Business and the Professions, University of Chicago.
- Senior technical writer under contract to Sprint. Developed the Sprint Proposal Library, which included writing and editing proposal materials, proposal boilerplate, forms, templates, technical manuals, technical requirements, and design reports. Also developed the following: an organized proposal library system, proposal sections for all offerings, sales presentations with product managers and marketing to place in the proposal library, white papers on core offerings, proposal boilerplate, capability statements, ➡

corporate overview boilerplate, and project plans.
- Editor and Writer for the Presentations Department: edited and wrote test reports, schedules, proposals (cost, logistics, technical, and executive volumes), promotional pieces, management and technical volumes.
- Strategized and wrote client newsletter, e-brochures, sales presentations, webinars, project descriptions, qualification statements, and other external communications.
- Copywrote a series of trade magazine ads discussing technology issues of "electronic post office" for collections industry.
- Developed communications strategies and marketing plans.
- Authored business proposals.
- Managed advertising, award submittals, and client relations program.
- Contributed monthly newsletter column on marketing and communication.
- Served as web editor responsible for writing and maintaining content, including service offering descriptions, value propositions, FAQs, news items, and seed content for online community.
- Managed content administration for web site, including updates, revisions, and posting of new material (ATG/Interwoven content management system).
- Redevelopment of web sites, including page design, site structure, and navigation.
- Researched, developed, and wrote web-based, interactive business training (included instructional story and material, quizzes and tutoring, expert interviews and audio, glossary and FAQs), conceptualized and worked with tech

staff to develop multimedia component that reinforced instructional material.

■ Developed informational resource articles on work/life issues. Identified new areas and ideas for development, including resources, tools, and potential alliance partners.

Writing/Editing

■ Research, drafting, and editing for book, Understanding Financial Statements: *A Journalist's Guide,* published by Marion Street Press.

■ Former teacher of writing seminars at Newberry Library and Latin School Adult Programs.

■ Author of nine articles that have appeared in national trade magazines, including the interviewing of subject matter experts.

■ Editor of employee newsletters.

■ Research, writing, and editing of public communications (policy statements, speeches, correspondence, and ceremonial messages).

■ Writing and editing reports (a client deliverable) covering investigative findings, conclusions, and recommendations.

Grant/Proposal Writing

■ Routinely researched, edited, and wrote a range of materials for corporations and not-for-profits, including:

Requests for Proposals (RFP), Requests for Information (RFI), and Requests for Qualifications (RFQ) for projects varying from $25,000 to $2 billion, with a 33 percent win ratio.

Responded to, prepared, and solicited documents above, analyzing and using sound judgment practices to select or identify opportunities, accuracy, appropriate capabilities, and content.

Identified and developed proposals, which resulted in three years of backlog (booked revenue stream) for URS Consultants.

Presentations and Graphic Design

- Designed presentations based upon determination of best response to client's needs, often working in a team environment.
- Led presentations to clients and trained marketing and project staff in making presentations.
- Developed multimedia presentations utilizing advanced software for use in large seminars and trade shows.
- Improved the response rate of sales and marketing materials by:

  Dramatically increasing the quality of PowerPoint presentations and Word documents through creative writing, formatting, and use of design elements, including tables and graphics (Excel charts, Visio diagrams, organization charts, logos, and images).

  Researching prospect business interests and creating material targeted to those interests.

Part Three

**Perfect Phrases
by Industry
and Discipline**

Advertising Director

Career Summaries

Creative, web-savvy Marketing and Advertising Executive with unparalleled ability to build advertising revenues in the Internet publishing market.

Exceptional skills in business development, including market definition, campaign design and implementation, and development of online services.

Key strengths in identifying and managing opportunities for strategic alliances, spotting trends in consumer markets, and anticipating emerging technologies.

Dynamic, inspirational leadership style, eliciting the best from creative contributors and sales support teams while meeting publication standards and deadlines.

Credited by executive management team for outstanding results in forecasting, budgeting, executive reporting, and project management.

Dynamic and proven professional with over 12 years marketing and advertising experience with demonstrated success in agency, consulting, and Fortune 1000 environments.

Acumen for developing solutions using the full complement of the marketing and promotional mix, inclusive of database, PR, sales promotion, events, and online channels.

Able to organize complex variables, build partnerships, then orchestrate internal and external resources toward shared objectives while maintaining clear communication and positive relationships. Possess self-initiative, an attention to detail, and a standard of excellence. ➡

Reputation for completing projects on time and in-budget with solutions focused on meeting marketing and promotional metrics, articulating strategic communications objectives, and maximizing production efficiencies.

Polished interpersonal and communications skills, with public speaking and presentation abilities. Wide range of computer systems and software knowledge and experience.

Manage an advertising operations support team of eight with a sales budget of $58 million.

Perfect Phrases
- Media Marketing Executive with 15 years of success in development and execution of strategies to position targeted cable network as "best in class" in reaching and influencing a niche market. Skilled at translating market intelligence into profitable business solutions. Extensive knowledge of the advertising sales and stewardship process.
- Areas of Expertise: Strategic Planning, Competitive Analysis and Positioning, Brand Management, Consumer Insights, Project Management, Media Planning, Staff Development and Training, and Profit Center Development.
- Create and continually improve a market-sensitive menu of strategic advertising options serving the diverse needs of e-commerce businesses across multiple industries.
- Foster strong business relationships with Fortune 250 clients. Act as advertising consultant to up-and-coming web and technology companies.
- Facilitate innovative, interactive territory meetings on a weekly basis. Set, and measured progress, toward team and individual objectives.

- Ranked number one among RCA's six global regions, 2003, 2004, and 2005. Grew key account base by 72 percent in first year, representing new revenues of $48 million.
- Promotion was recognized by executive leadership in a press release: "Samantha has consistently achieved major gains in advertising revenues by positioning iWORLD as the number one Internet news destination for executives." —Kevin Talon, VP of Marketing for RCA
- Fashion and entertainment industry Advertising Production Specialist. Extensive credentials in key account sales, marketing, and management.
- Produce, cast, negotiate, and budget photo shoots for multimillion-dollar domestic and international accounts. Coordinate and execute worldwide photo shoots. Direct 20 to 40 international production teams. Engineer and maintain high-profile fashion photographers. Cast, book, and schedule leading models and performers.
- Open and retain million-dollar accounts, including Verizon, NBC, KKR, and Acushnet (Titleist Golf). Supervise departmental staff of 15.
- Supervise 25 employees in the page layout and printing of syndicated comics, newspaper articles, and puzzles for national newspapers. Oversee weekly page makeup and client contact for personal ads in 15 nationwide publications. Manage electronic pre-press section. Schedule and quality-check four-color promotional ads for licensing, sales, and comic art departments. Set prep quality standards. Design and quality-check covers for syndicated newspaper TV guides.
- Department is nationally recognized as leader in in-house printing.

- Developed concepts and designs for clients in the film, theater, nonprofit, and fashion industries. Designed special promotional material, direct-mail brochures, press kits, and corporate identities. Produced exceptional quality work for clients on a tight budget and a tight deadline.
- Designed newspaper ads for real estate companies, stores, restaurants, and politicians.

Attorney

Note: Look at the tone of the phrases used, the type of subject matter. Of particular interest is the phrase below that objectively describes the attorney's compensation plan, hours worked, and his or her contribution to the firm.

Career Summaries

Fifteen-year partner in busy corporate and consumer bankruptcy and commercial litigation practice. Representation of various businesses in collections, contract drafting and negotiation, SEC issues, financing, leasing, commercial loan drafting and review, loan workouts, asset-based financing, master-factoring agreements, liquidations, receiverships, and assignment for the benefit of creditors

Representation of corporations in successful Chapter 11 reorganizations, including contentious in-court legal proceedings, complex negotiations with secured creditors and creditors' committees, as well as regular briefings with senior officials/executives of the involved entities. Drafting of intricate legal and business documents and ability to communicate said documents clearly in court under litigious situations.

Manage client relationships and develop and implement business strategies to promote the financial development of the firm. Oversee associate development and work-product as well as all matters related to staffing, budgeting, resource utilization, and office administration. Daily utilization and enhancement of managerial and organization skills, in addition to the ability to handle ongoing multiple projects while maintaining a sharp attention to detail.

Twenty-one years experience in U.S. and international business development and technology commercialization efforts relating to space exploration by integrating fully and applying the following experiences:

Eighteen years of patent and other intellectual property, legal, and business experience in a broad array of complex technologies.

Ten years of combined civil service and Navy Reserve experience in defense systems development and acquisition.

Six years of active duty Navy Submarine Force service as a nuclear trained line officer focusing on the new construction of a fast attack nuclear submarine.

Perfect Phrases

- Annual Salary: $350,000. Hours worked per week: 75. Supervisor: Victor Hinojosa, Intellectual Property Section Lead Attorney (Columbus, OH). Recruited to serve as Partner in Intellectual Property Law tasked with assisting in establishing firm's Dayton, Ohio, office. Firm size: 525 attorneys.
- Initiated and managed expansion of office file for national law firm.
- Increased business for office expansion by 300 percent.
- Progressive expertise in trial law involving catastrophic injuries and complex commercial issues.
- Oversaw billing on regular basis, utilizing innovative software word processing program.
- Managed trials of commercial and personal injury claims with 100 percent success.
- Point person in associate development for multimillion-dollar billings.
- Oversaw establishment and provided management of associate training program.

- Provided consultation to products manufacturers regarding proposed safety changes.
- Experienced in alternative dispute resolution.
- Representation of various banks/businesses in security agreements, commercial loan workouts, contract negotiation, UCC issues, loan drafting and review, regulatory matters, asset-based financing, master-factoring agreements, liquidations, receiverships, and assignments for the benefit of creditors.
- Detailed experience in corporate reorganizations, creditors' rights, and commercial litigation. Representation of secured and unsecured creditors, creditors' committees, debtors, equity holders, and trustees in all phases of proceedings under the United States Bankruptcy Code.
- Drafted and successfully confirmed debtor's plan of reorganization for multimillion-dollar company in Chapter 11 proceeding. Settled client's claim against large trading card company, which included complex negotiations with Major League Baseball, the National Football League, and the National Hockey League.
- Solo practitioner with a diversified caseload of real estate transactions and litigation, business transactions and litigation, corporate and partnership matters, estate planning, probate, bankruptcy, and mortgage foreclosures.
- Real estate transactions and litigation, business transactions and litigation, corporate and partnership matters, estate planning, bankruptcy, mortgage foreclosures, and homeowner associations.
- Worked closely with CEO and COO to define new organizational structure and drive standardization throughout the organization.

➡

- Developed policies and procedures, job descriptions, pay scales, and produced first Employee Handbook.
- Credited for taking little known health-care company and making it employer of choice by formalizing corporate culture and leading internal/external branding/communications campaigns. Established HR and Legal Services as strategic partner with corporate leaders and Facility Administrators.
- Standardized hiring and training program and spearheaded strategy to attract medical personnel in extremely competitive market.
- Challenged in last 12 months to drive employee morale in the face of management reorganization from six partners to one. Collaborated with executive and field management to support downsizing, including nearly 50 percent of corporate staff and roughly $1M in combined field staff reductions. Led communications program to employees and ensured compliance with HR policies to avoid legal issues and complaints.
- Counseled management and used legal expertise to thwart lawsuits and threats, defeating all employment-related complaints with zero dollars used for settlements or legal fees. Maintained strict oversight of outside legal counsel, closely monitoring strategy and cost.

Banking

Career Summary

Devise and implement innovative marketing principles and promotional sales events for commercial and consumer projects to further support financial growth.

Counsel high-net-worth individuals and corporate clients with regard to investment opportunities, risk analysis, and monetary returns.

Cross-sell banking services and products to clientele.

Participate in community events to position the bank as a leader within the territory.

Senior Operating Executive in the banking industry with proven leadership skills and expertise in refining credit quality, returns on investment and capital, cross-marketing, asset growth, and analysis of risk-adjusted returns on mortgage lending. Successfully orchestrated the centralization of lending, collections, underwriting, and loan-processing procedures to maximize asset performance. Early background includes regional operations and training management for a St. Louis–based investment company, supervising offices in 12 midwestern states.

Recruited to bolster the lending operation for community bank established in 1956, now serving 25,000 customers with $170 million in total deposits.

Centralized the Collection and Secondary Mortgage departments. Sold real estate loans in the Secondary Market totaling more than $20 million from 1993 to 1995. Collection of recovery accounts exceeded charge-offs for the last three years.

Increased loan outstanding from $63 to $106 million.

Decreased classified loans from $10 to $3 million.

Implemented an indirect lending department now serving more than 3,000 loan customers.

Perfect Phrases

- Reduced retail delinquency from 4.45 percent in 2003 to 1.79 percent in 2005.
- Assumed additional responsibility of servicing all commercial collections deemed a Workout Status. Accepted the responsibility of managing the bank's Other Retail Estate Owned (ORE). Reduced ORE from $1.1 million to $700,000.
- Centralized the Indirect Lending area into a single location servicing 46 auto dealers in the Metro-East area. With two underwriters and a clerical staff of four, processed more than 1,000 applications each month. Purchased $11 million in auto loan paper in the first three months of 1993 for a net gain in outstanding of $3 million.
- With the centralization of the collection department, reduced the amount of charge-offs from 1.67 percent in 1991 to 0.85 percent in 1992.
- Centralized all Direct Lending into a single department processing approximately 200 direct loan applications per month. Provided a centralized approval process for Central Bank's 11 locations.
- Successfully organized and set up a Secondary Mortgage Department for Central Bank in 1989. Originally started this effort as the sole underwriter for FNMA. Formulated a staff that grew the department to $12 million in FNMA loans and serviced direct real estate loans totaling $60 million. FNMA delinquency was zero when I left Central Bank.
- Generated over $100,000 in revenue and fee income within a four-month period.

➡

- Branch Manager with 17 years of progressively responsible positions in the financial industry. Strong managerial, administrative, interpersonal, and problem-solving skills, with proven leadership ability. Directed daily operations for retail bank, including branch sales, business development, customer service, and credit analysis. Managed staff of 15 Customer Service Representatives and Tellers.
- Manage operations, personnel, budget, profit planning, and audit and compliance for branch with assets up to $19 million. Proven ability to achieve success given difficult situations. Turned around Mason branch within three months, bringing branch within audit compliance. Maintained excellent audit ratings. Effectively managed branch throughout merger process. Able to plan, organize, delegate, administer, and direct in order to meet branch goals and corporate mission.
- Sales Team Leader; strong customer service orientation. Of 79 offices, Mason Branch was number one in Cross-Sell Ratio for 1990. As individual, placed second in Cross-Sell for that same year. Outstanding achievement in Cross-Sell Ratio for 1992. Increased branch average monthly deposit balance by $1.5 million from 1992 to 1993.
- Strong leadership skills with the ability to generate enthusiasm among staff. Supervised, developed, and directed staff of seven. Determined staffing levels and reorganized job responsibilities to effectively utilize resources during merger. Implemented a Retail Sales Performance System to train employees to be part of sales culture.
- Named "Rookie of the Year," for most productive new teller, 2005.

➥

- Recognized for highest level of accuracy of all 18 tellers, 2006.
- Significantly expanded bank's community development efforts through increased involvement with local, state, and federal programs (SBA). This resulted in new inroads to more complex, nontraditional business opportunities, which yielded profitability as well as greater market penetration and share for United Bank & Trust.
- Increased 2005 commercial loan closings over 2004 through aggressive promotion and marketing; personally responsible for developing and managing capital investment programs for approximately 45 Cincinnati businesses.
- Effectively promoted visibility of United Bank & Trust through planning and presentation of seminars for clients and through participation at conferences and trade shows.
- Managed promotion and sales of complete breadth of financial products and services to portfolio of 60 clients characterized by high net worth. Responsibilities included origination, underwriting, and closing of commercial/consumer loans.
- Successfully restructured entire $3.2MM portfolio in noncompliance with bank loan policy.
- Managed $8MM loan portfolio for savings bank with assets of $7 billion. Oversaw new business development, financial data collection, and analysis.
- Elected to bank officer's position to assist in formation and establishment of commercial bank.
- Managed consumer/mortgage lending department, generating $12MM in consumer loans and $6MM in commercial loans for fiscal year 2005.

Biotechnology

Career Summary

Management professional attuned to the ever-changing needs of business. Extremely service-oriented, with a unique combination of intuitive and analytical abilities. Astute in identifying market plan needs, creating actionable programs, and effectively interacting with the sales field.

Robust analytical and problem-solving skills.

Methodical, investigative, and creative.

Specialized in the physicochemical and mechanical characterization of solids.

Knowledgeable in formulation science, physical pharmacy, and analytical chemistry.

Well-acquainted with most of the instruments and techniques used today, such as UV, FT-IR, HPLC, DSC/TGA, powder X-ray diffractometry, scanning electron microscopy, light microscopy, VTI water sorption analyzer, GMP dissolution, BET surface analyzer, and helium pycnometer, among others.

Experienced in solid dosage form design and development.

Perfect Phrases

- Carried out preformulation studies for new drug applicants. Conducted formulation studies of various dosage forms.
- Performed HPLC assay method development, prevalidation, and validation studies, and prepared the corresponding reports.
- Carried out stability and excipient compatibility studies and completed the related reports.
- Analyzed in-process samples, cleaning equipment

samples, and finished pharmaceuticals to ensure quality, uniformity, and safety of products.

- Experienced lab data and record keeping, lab logs maintenance, purchase orders, equipment maintenance/calibration, and hazardous waste management.
- Practiced current Good Manufacturing Practices and Good Laboratory Procedures (cGMP and cGLP) to execute projects and to report the same.
- Updated the master batch records for most of the pharmaceutical products and elaborated SOPs.
- Supervised packaging processes and experienced managing personnel.
- Poster Presentations/Honors/Awards:

  Pharmacy Graduate Program Excellence Award, Michigan State University (2003-2004).

  Graduate Student Travel Award, Michigan State University (2004).

  Graduate Student Travel Award, Michigan State University (2003).

  Graduate Student Travel Award, Michigan State University (2002).

  John Lach Fellowship, Michigan State University (2000).

- As a practicing scientist trained in mammalian biology, molecular cell biology, virology, microbiology, and molecular genetics, led R&D scientists in the support and service of pharmaceuticals discovery. The management and administrative skills gained in industry were further refined while establishing a state research institute, and

➡

then in a start-up biotech company. The process of scientific discovery and promoting practical applications of good science continue to be my interest.

- Managed the design and development of knowledge-based products for modeling complex biological interactions.
- Performed senior management team responsibilities, including business development, marketing, and M&A analyses in the biotechnology and pharmaceuticals sectors.
- Developed strategic plans to promote the adoption of biosimulation products and services within pharmaceuticals discovery and preclinical research.
- Molecular Biology of Inflammatory Mediators.
- Identified human genes responding to antiinflammatory drugs via differential display.
- Cloned and expressed novel metalloproteinases using unique reporter systems.
- Identified drug targets through SAGE, differential display, and database mining.
- Developed novel gene-family cloning systems, activity (expression) cloning systems, and cell-based assays to find disease-related proteases.
- Management of Biotechnology Research. Simultaneously supervised two groups that combined; formed a 52-person research organization dedicated to produce molecular and cellular reagents as a service:

    Supervised 28 scientists (11 direct reports—eight Ph.D.s) who provided cell and molecular biology support for five drug discovery groups. Technologies: gene acquisition expression cloning, PCR, subtraction libraries), recombinant protein expression (bacterial, ➡

yeast, insect, mammalian), bioinformatics, and protein engineering. Core service facilities: oligonucleotide synthesis, cytometry, and DNA sequencing.

- Biotechnology Resources Group: led 24 scientists (six direct reports—five Ph.D.s) who provided companywide support in scale-up protein purification, protein analysis, fermentation, large-scale cell production, and monoclonal antibody production.
- Duties at Merck & Co. included scale-up and scale-down experiments in fermentation/pilot-plant. Extensive work with HPLC, including Perkin Elmer and TSP models using turbochrom software.
- Worked with fermentation processes in the development of pharmaceuticals.
- Hands on work with one-liter BioFlo 2000 glass fermentors, as well as 5- and 70-liter Biotech International steel fermentors in preparation for scale-up. Experience with centrifugation, including ultracentrifuge. Provided an intermediate level of analytical support for raw materials and in-process product testing. Familiar with GMP environment.

Chief Executive Officer

Career summaries

Executive Summary

Telecommunications executive with over 30 years successful industry experience in Executive Leadership, Product/Process Development, Strategic Marketing/Sales, and Operations. Strong leader with extensive knowledge of wireless communications and cutting edge network technologies. Proven record of building revenues, increasing profitability, building strong customer relationships and establishment of solid operations in the wireless communications industry. Visionary leader, able to bring organization, creative thinking, and innovative problem solving to bear on business operations. Inspirational manager of talent teams.

Career Profile

Seven years experience as CEO for Fortune 500 consumer products company.

Twenty-three years in consumer products and packaging.

Over 14 years related business management and marketing experience, with a proven track record in building, supporting, and managing relationships across functional teams and corporate hierarchies.

Experience in leading and managing successful organizations B2B and stewarding new marketing projects and proposals.

Supervised, coordinated, oversaw, and represented complete marketing and advertising initiatives for publication and media for the community at large, and monitored all press-released and printed material for distribution over 200-mile radius.

Entrepreneurial experience in managing and marketing new business development, including finance, start-up operations, and successful turnarounds.

Perfect Phrases

- Built initial sales force, increasing run rate share for web hosting from 30 percent to over 46 percent.

    Launched worldwide hosted exchange business through strategic agreement with Verizon.

    Led strategic agreement with Korea Telecom (KT), leading to $465MM in new revenue.

    Directed development of and go-to-market partnerships for hosted unified communications solution.

- Managed large organizations with 450 employees internationally, including senior staff of subsidiaries. Managed operating budgets up to $50 MM.

- As CEO, contributed vision, strategy, and leadership with full P&L accountability for all aspects of operations. Led a core executive team of 10—CFO, Director of HR, Director of Development, CTO, Director of Product Management, Director of Quality, Support Manager, Director of Marketing, North American Sales Manager, European Sales Manager—and provided indirect oversight to thousands of other employees.

- As Chief Marketing Officer, led all aspects of market research, as well as target market trend sampling. Led Product Planning Specification development, Prototype Alpha/Beta end user testing, and user documentation. Working with both internal and external resources, led total branding effort, including company and product names, along with all supporting web presence and sales support tools leading to European and North American market introductions. Led efforts to attract and secure new Growth Phase VC/Private Equity Investors.

- Three years at a top-tier venture capital firm, T. Rowe Growth Funds (TRGF), as a Co-Managing Director of a $457 million fund.
- Helped start a new technology fund: deal flow, business plans, due diligence, investments, portfolio, and boards.
- Two years working with private equity firms when with a consulting firm, PwC: helped with due diligence and structuring deals exceeding $200 million.
- Structured Venture Capital (VC), Leverage Buy-Out (LBO), Initial Public Offering (IPO), and Merger and Acquisition (M&A) deals.
- Helped raise over $600 million in debt and equity for a public company Start-Up and Corporate/Business Development Experience.
- Education Experience:

    Harvard Business School (HBS) MBA—Alumni Network—for two years.

    Scored highest In Accounting and Finance at HBS.

    GE Financial Management Program classes for 2 1/2 years.

    Michigan State University (MSU): Finance and Accounting B.A. for four years.

    Taught Strategic Planning course at GE.

- High technology senior executive experienced in identifying market opportunities, raising capital, building teams, developing new products, forming enterprises/start-ups, and affecting turnarounds.

- Industry experience focused on the Internet, information, communication, entertainment, and transaction services.

- Recent experience with Internet services in the U.S. and Asia Pacific, competitive local exchange carriers, interactive television, cable television, electronic commerce, merger and acquisitions, initial public offerings, data mining, terrestrial navigation systems, and computer-telephony integration.

- Previous experience in electronic banking, electronic brokerage, retail, consumer packaged goods, automotive, airlines, advertising, management information systems, and decision support systems.

- Managed a direct staff of 10 with a total complement of 758 full-time employees and an annual operating budget of $90 million. Approximately 30 percent of the hospital employees are under collective bargaining agreements.

- Responsible for total operations of this 266-bed community general hospital, providing acute care services as well as open heart surgery, OB, NICU, in- and outpatient psychiatry, home care, sleep lab, pain management, wound care, and others. Facilities include an independent outpatient surgery center and a medical office building.

- CEO and President, with a track record of leadership and fast-growth through strategic/tactical execution:

    Grew four companies from early stages to mid-cap size—two approaching $400M per annum.

    Career history primarily in Enterprise Software: Licensed Business Process.

➥

- Company Lifecycle/Event exposure includes: start-up, M&A, restructure, turnaround, IPO, and Public.

    Led pursuit, sales capture, and delivery management of over $3.9 billion in new business since 1985.

    Directed multiple go-to-market sales and marketing initiatives: direct and indirect channels, alliances, and JVs.

    Successfully executed seven mergers and acquisitions and four investment solicitations and road shows.

    Profiled in a 2005 CEO conference as "One of the Best CEOs You May Never Have Heard of": "A rare talent for translating vision into strategic focus with fast-paced tactical execution; a transformational leadership style that empowers organizational effectiveness and high-energy team-building; a hands-on, proactive management style that combines aggressive business momentum with increasing net profits, creating results and rewards for both the employees and shareholders alike."

Database or Data Processing

Career Summaries

Data Warehouse Manager offering 10 years of experience and in-depth knowledge of the functional and data needs of e-businesses.

Data warehouse development experience incorporates skills in programming, analysis, architecture, and project management. Expertise in high-level and detailed system design, requirements gathering, logical and physical data modeling, development, and implementation. Expert knowledge of data modeling in ERP and other major application areas.

Well-versed in Oracle (Oracle Express, Oracle Reporter, Oracle Financial), Oracle tools, and Erwin products. Data migration experience using Informatica, C++, Java, Corba, multidimensional database, JavaScript, Oracle web server, and Java. Exceptional use of CASE tools as part of an overall development effort.

Extensive knowledge of DBMS: Oracle RDBMS, SQL, PL/SQL, STAR Schema Modeling. Experienced in UNIX operating system, Microsoft PC operating systems including NT, desktop productivity software, and client/server system architecture.

Proven ability to assemble and mobilize project teams, building consensus among multidisciplinary technical and functional teams in the rapid development and implementation of data warehousing solutions. Recognized by managers and colleagues as a strong, positive leader and a sharp strategic thinker.

Data Mining Specialist: Developing Solutions for Online Relationship Marketing.

➡

Specialist in developing customer affinity through the design, implementation, and management of data mining solutions for relationship marketing applications. Full life-cycle experience on enterprise-scale data warehousing/mining projects. Strong team leader and results-focused manager. Capabilities include:

Data Warehousing, Mining, and Reporting	Mass Marketing Communication Tools
Data Analysis and Knowledge Discovery	Systems Design and Development
CRM Technologies and Tools	Web-Enabled Decision Support Applications

Perfect Phrases

- Drive the strategic vision and evolution from centralized data warehouse to distributed data marts. Report to divisional IT management with accountability for global processes. Manage a budget of $5.6 million.
- Provide guidance to software development teams on the use and purpose of data warehouses. Direct a team of seven data warehouse developers/analysts in the daily operations of the corporate data warehouse. Oversee all aspects of the warehouses, including data sourcing, data migration, data quality, data warehouse design, and implementation.
- Scope, plan, and prioritize multiple project deliverables, based on data warehousing dependencies and changing business needs. Develop project plans, identify and fill project resource needs, and manage projects to on-time, on-budget completion.

- Influence tool-set and business needs assessment. Lead the selection of third-party software; manage vendor relationships. Successfully manage multiple projects in the design and implementation of warehouse functionality and interfaces.
- Translated an enterprise data model, created dimension and fact tables to support budgeting, financial planning, analysis, and dataware systems, in collaboration with the DBA and Data Steward.
- Determined database/data mart business requirements. Created the logical and physical database/datamart design for Relational and OLAP Data Warehouse environment.

Computer Technology

Hardware: Main Frames, IBM 360/370, Mini Computers, RISC6000, AS400, PCs, and peripherals

Connectivity: Novel NetWare, LAN, WAN, Windows NT, 95, NT's Workstation

Languages: Assembler, C, C++, COBOL, FORTRAN, PL/I, Visual Basic, Basic

Relational Data Base: SQL (Relational Data Base), Informix, SQL Server, FOX Pro

Operating Systems: AIX, UNIX, XENIX, DOS, DOS VS, OS, OS VS, LAN, and WAN

Database Manager and Director of Information Systems of the SW Division. Recruited to assume Director, Information Systems position. Scope of responsibility includes management of all systems. Primary responsibilities involve creating ➡

new systems based upon client needs. Ancillary duties involve enhancing, servicing, and maintaining existing systems applications for new customers. Oversee daily activities of a Network Administrator and three Systems Administrators, and seven PC Support, Computer Operators, and Data Processing Clerks. Primary duties include identifying specific needs of each department, determining feasibility, and assigning systems administrators to accomplish.

- Achieved $78 million increase in annual sales ($322 to $400 million) by eliminating systems down time, increasing availability of systems time, and increasing customer computers, allowing 24-hour-a-day usage.
- Led focus group that created systems designed to eliminate an average three hours down time. Monitored and modified systems, achieving weekly labor costs savings of $72K.
- Developed a program that monitors systems every 10 minutes to identify "problems" prior to development and allowing preventive action to eliminate down time.
- Expedited sales orders processing by providing 200-plus laptops to sales persons. Implemented direct order entry systems to expedite sales process.
- Developed and implemented an Electronic Data Input (EDI) ordering system for U.S. Navy within six weeks. Achieved $25 million annual order from Navy by meeting the established deadline.

Review the development, testing, and implementation of data and application security plans, products, and control techniques to ensure the security of clients' personal and sensitive credit card information being transmitted via the web. Control access to data and change passwords. ➡

Thoroughly investigate and recommend appropriate corrective actions for data and application security incidents. Identify data security risks and report breaches. Lead and direct staff to scan all application and production software environments.

Technically proficient with Firewalls, Virus Detection Software, and web site checking platforms. Evaluate and test security and virus detection software. Work closely with the administrator to monitor the system for intrusions.

Develop Security Tools
Designed and implemented a highly effective data and computer operations security checklist for daily use by computer operators. The result was a decrease in noted security deficiencies of 11 percent in less than six months.

Designed and incorporated a tiered level of access to databases, creating a "hacker-proof/need to know" security measure environment.

Implement Security Contingency Plans
Drafted an Intrusion Response Plan: implemented the plan during a real-life security crisis—every computer database was infected with a contagious virus that deleted data files. Directed operators to follow protocol, and operations resumed within three hours.

Drafted a Disaster Recovery Plan: wrote and implemented a procedures manual to ensure the security of data through off-site storage measures and theft avoidance, including contingency plans for natural disasters or terrorist attacks.

Technical Qualifications
Extensive experience in design and construction of data warehousing and processing systems.

➡

Oracle Certified Professional—DBA; extensive Oracle PL/SQL qualifications.

In-depth understanding of OLAP, data mining, and ad-hoc query tools.

Experienced in UNIX/Perl scripting; C and C++ software development abilities.

Highly proficient with most popular reporting tools: Actuate, Crystal Reports, and Cognos.

Advanced skills with data analysis applications: SAS and SPSS.

Deep understanding of CRM tools: Epiphany, Broadbase, and Siebel eConfigurator.

Knowledgeable in strategies for linking data to web content management platforms.

Finance and Accounting

Career Summaries

Certified Public Accountant/Chief Financial Officer with 18 years experience in corporate accounting and 10 years experience in multicorporation accounting operations in the medical field. Areas of expertise include:

  Financial Administration/Reporting
  Operations Management
  Telecommunications Integration
  Multicorporation/Partnership Taxes
  Acquisitions/Joint Ventures
  Credit Lines/Administration
  Accounting Systems Design/Implementation
  Central Accounting Administration
  Financial Planning/Analysis
  Acquisition Negotiations
  Premium Rate Strategies
  Equipment Leasing/Portfolio
  Multisite Retail Purchasing/Negotiations
  Strategic Planning/Budgeting

Corporate Finance/Accounting/Administration/MIS

Sixteen-year professional career directing domestic and international corporate finance for challenging and complex operations. Expert negotiation and transaction management qualifications. Skilled decision maker, problem solver, and team leader. Fluent in French and Scandinavian languages. Conversational German.

  Merger and Acquisition Management
  Corporate Divestiture and Realignment

Strategic Planning and Development
SEC Regulatory Affairs and Documentation
Securities and Investment Banking
Public Relations and Investor Relations
Financial Consolidation and Reporting
Asset and Liability Management
General Accounting Operations
Operations and Financial Analysis
Pension and Benefits Administration
Domestic and International Tax

Perfect Phrases

- Led financial team to orchestrate five major acquisitions in last three years valued at over $325 million each. Entities involved include Cisco Systems, Aramark Services, Cadbury Schweppes, Nokia, and Frito-Lay.
- Prepared comprehensive financial analysis, reviews, and recommendations for acquiring company and subsidiaries.
- Joined early stage company to provide financial and investment leadership to accelerate growth, expansion, and diversification. Focused efforts on developing investor and banking relationships, strengthening corporate business infrastructure, introducing sound financial policies, and implementing advanced information technologies. Supervised organization of 34 people.
- Advised CEO, CFO, and board directors on a wide range of strategic and business planning, finance accounting, and corporate development and acquisition activities.
- Directed all tax work for all 12 corporations and performed all accounting, financial, and tax planning for David Faulk and his family members. Prepared over 400 Federal/State individual and corporate tax returns annually.

- Saved Atlas Transit Inc. over $250,000 in tax accounting fees. Saved the firm over $400,000 by studying and adjusting the depreciation state allocation method.
- Analyzed financial status of London office and recommended its closure. Revenues increased and operational efficiencies improved concurrently with these cost cuts.
- Managed accounting department consisting of A/P, A/R, cost management, and general ledger maintenance.
- Saved the firm over $190,000 by successfully negotiating insurance rates. Also saved the company $100,000 in credit card processing fees. Implemented a 401(k) plan. Streamlined monthly reporting period from 60 to 40 days.
- Managed team with responsibility for all areas of operations and accounting including: budgeting, cash management, monthly financial statements, account controls, year-end accounting/audit preparation, and personnel supervision.
- Instrumental in the research and coordination to integrate voice, data, and fax over data lines that will save $100 to $200K in long distance charges annually.
- Saved $87K in annual corporate management salaries through comprehensive management of the financial programs and credit administration of the group.
- Designed, implemented, and managed all centralized accounting, management information systems, and internal control policies and procedures for 11 corporations.
- Instrumental in the negotiation and acquisition of $3 million home-care and retail pharmacy stores; negotiated a $14 million contract for pharmaceuticals resulting in a

➡

savings of 1.5 to 3 percent on cost of goods for each retail store.

- Responsible for the accurate and timely processing of accounts payable/receivable, payroll (48 employees), insurance and union reports, and sales tax/payroll tax reporting for this $2.1 million firm. Performed job costing, account analysis, and general ledger management using Excel.

- Freed up $32,000 by reducing A/R aging from 77 to 38 days.

- Trained and directed six employees in accounting department. Analyzed and interpreted forecasts, capital expenditures, and financial data for $3.2 million manufacturer. Directly involved in budget preparation and cash flow.

- Provided financial data and accounting services in connection with change in ownership, including licensing requirements, conversion from S corp. to C corp., and collaboration with attorney.

- Reduced primary expense category from 50 percent to 34 to 36 percent, saving company approximately $1.2 million through implementation of purchasing controls.

- Instrumental in the implementation of monthly credit reports of each account being forwarded to sales force; enabled comprehension of account's creditworthiness and future sales tactics.

- As Director, held full responsibility for directing all accounting operations and monitoring financial performance of each operating division. Defined MIS information requirements to meet operating needs, and established corporatewide accounting policies, procedures, and reporting packages. Led a professional staff of 16 (11 of whom were CPAs with Big Six experience) with dotted line responsibility for 70-plus Division and Group Controllers.

■ Established the entire accounting and financial infrastructure for new corporation. Developed policies and procedures for budgeting, financial analysis, financial reporting, tax accounting, and pension accounting. Coordinated with Treasury Department for international cash management.

■ Directed complex financial analysis and integration of all accounting and financial operations for 19 acquisitions worldwide ($500,000 to $258 million). Integrated two acquisitions concurrent with company spin-off.

■ Developed economic analysis of impact on stock price of share buyback versus acquisition investment with the company's price/earnings ratio as measure.

■ Successfully represented Williams in an arbitration of a disputed sales contract. Presented and interpreted financial and contractual documentation for the court, and recovered $20.6 million of disputed $21 million for the corporation.

■ Coordinated and implemented all aspects of general bookkeeping. Reconciled bank statements and accounts. Utilized chart of accounts to code vouchers and entered accounts payable invoices. Prepared cash disbursements, applied cash receipts, researched bills, checked batches and day reports for accuracy. Generated computerized end-of-month reports. Utilized trial balance for various schedules.

Fund-raising

Career Summary

Started, organized, and managed nonprofit campaigns for 10 years.

Headed national capital initiatives for a national nonprofit for six years, raising more than $20 million.

Executive Director experience at both local and national levels.

Experienced in Economic Development studies and campaigns for Chambers of Commerce, government entities, and Economic Development commissions.

Experienced in self-employment and independent, on-site work.

An individual whose personal philosophy and values have enabled him to succeed and to inspire and lead others.

Perfect Phrases

- As a senior officer, started, organized, and managed multimillion-dollar economic initiatives.
- Experienced as a campaign consultant in: Feasibility Studies, Volunteer Development, seven-figure investment development.
- Managed significant Chamber campaigns all under budget and over goal. Oversaw all systems and operational issues with clients and my team.
- Built on existing Volunteer Development to increase over 50 percent.
- The South Texas program alone raised over $250,000 and gained 5,000 volunteers. Personally volunteered in the program for 15 years, including coaching. Established statewide partnership with the ATP of America and the

➡

First Serve Program. Provided staff support on capital initiatives for handicap accessible parks and buildings.

- Training: for several years, a trainer in development on the executive level. Trained at both the professional and volunteer levels. Extensive public and seminar experience. Presented to groups of 40 to 300. Trained in resource development, planned giving, major gifts, volunteer development, and capital campaigns.
- Responsible for the formation and incorporation of an all-volunteer 501(c)3 charitable organization, including corporate charter, articles of incorporation, IRS status request generation, and internal procedure definitions. Successfully completed state, federal, and local registration for organization with gross income over $100K by second year. Successfully negotiated rent-free associations with pet supply businesses for pet-adoption locations.
- Successfully defined volunteer roles and attracted volunteers to grow from three volunteers at our inception to a current status of 50-plus volunteers with a database of over 3,000 supporters with current Volunteer Campaign under way.
- Successfully conceived and oversaw the various fund-raising campaigns that have enabled us to operate in the black since inception. Successfully developed newsletters (current circulation 4,000), database, internal documentation, and externally focused literature.
- Raised over $4.2 million in past five years.
- Five-year consistent record of attaining projected fund-raising targets.
- Reduced volunteer turnover of 38 percent to less than 8 percent annually. Increased donations 123 percent.

Hospitality: Hotel

Career Summary

General Manager: accomplished Hotel Executive with 20 years experience in food service field; hold distinguished FMP credential.

Consistent track record of successfully turning around faltering operations and creating profitability and excellence; utilize keen assessment and problem-solving abilities, dynamic training techniques, and key motivational strategies that build accountability and enhance staff performance.

Flexible, adaptable style and hands-on approach; a skilled manager who thrives in an atmosphere demanding excellence, autonomy, and strong team-building skills.

Possess highly polished communication and interpersonal skills.

Graduate of several of Europe's premier hotel management/culinary institutions; professional management experience acquired through employment with some of Europe's most prestigious establishments as well as a Boston four-diamond hotel; multilingual fluency includes English, German, and French.

Perfect Phrases

- Responsibilities include management and relationship building of over 60 corporate accounts worth over $1 million in 2002. Liaison between account decision makers and the hotel in negotiating corporate room rates. Solicitation efforts resulting in six new accounts worth over $60,000 in 2002. Averaging 10 outside sales calls and entertainments per week to build and maintain client relationships.

➡

- Responsible for the following markets: Texas, SW Sports, and TX universities. Accountable for approximately $1.4 million in guest-room revenues in last three quarters of 2003, and exceeded yearly goal by $310,000. Maintain aggressive solicitation process to increase new business within the Texas market. Assisted in the preparation of annual forecast and marketing plan. Forecast group room nights and rates for all definite business within territory. Specializing in sports and small corporate meeting negotiations. Built and established relationships through ongoing entertainment, sales calls, site visits, and trade shows.
- Responsible for the following channel markets for the Ritz-Carlton, Atlanta, and the Ritz-Carlton, Buckhead: Small Group Corporate, Sports, and Universities. Accountable for approximately $1.3 million in guest-room revenues in 2004 and exceeded first quarter goal by 10 percent. Maintain aggressive solicitation process to increase new business within the local Atlanta market. Assisted in the preparation of the following: Annual Forecast, Marketing Plan, and conversion to Delphi. Forecast group room nights and rates for all definite business within territory. Specializing in sports and small corporate meeting negotiations. Built and established relationships through ongoing entertainment, sales calls, site visits, and trade shows.
- Responsible for the creation of all service concepts, training, and hiring of all employees prior to the opening of the hotel in 2002. Responsible for overseeing all aspects of the Rooms Division operation. Also in charge of initiating and maintaining and vending relations.
- Responsible for writing the entire hotel room club and penthouse unit's integration operating processes. First

integration of its type for the Hilton hotel company.

- Created operational room's budget for 2003 and 2004.
- Set up and developed all departmental training programs for all rooms division departments. Instrumental in training all employees on these programs.
- Participation on the weekly new hire orientation "Basic's" presentations.
- In charge of planning, modifying, and disseminating operational logistics on a daily basis and coordinating efforts with all departments to ensure flawless customer service.
- Oversee all hotel operations in the absence of the General Manager.
- Set and refine all seasonal staffing levels to maximize profitability levels.
- Effectively developed a succession planning program for the division, where seven management/supervisory positions were all filled internally, while still maintaining guest satisfaction scores.
- Exceeded 9/10 guest satisfaction score goals in the opening year of business.
- Exceeded 95 percent Rooms Division employee satisfaction in first year of operation. Third highest hotel within the United States.
- Fifteen years experience in hotel management and operations.
- Ability to motivate employees to achieve and exceed individual and group expectations.
- Experienced in the planning and implementation of effective policies, procedures, training, and staff development.

➡

- Increased comment card returns by 20 percent through guest recognition program.
- Operated a Rooms Division payroll at 17 percent to revenue for six months.
- Improved revenue and occupancy 29 percent over previous year.
- Oversee the 617-room full-service convention hotel with 58,000 square feet of meeting space. In the process of reorganizing the management structure. Redeploying the sales effort to increase RevPar and Market Share.
- Managed the operation of a 285-room full-service convention hotel with 31,000 square feet of meeting space. Since arrived, increased market share from 79 to 124 percent, RevPar by 28 percent, and rooms sold by 25 percent.
- Competitive set decreased by 7 percent for the same period. Increased the GOP $1.5 million. Selected "Best Hotel" by *Reader's Choice* for 2002 and 2003.
- Responsible for the financial oversight of this $800-million development project. Revamped all systems and controls for this project. Project consisted of 1,000-room Convention Hotel, 220,000 square feet of meeting space, 60 room Five-Star Country Club, 18-hole golf course, 11 tennis courts, marina, and 50,000-square-foot European Spa.
- Hired as second-in-command for the project. Finalized all budgets and economic modeling for the project. Point person between operations and the asset managers.
- Managed the operation of a 225-suite full-service resort with 10,000 square feet of meeting space. Repositioned the resort within the marketplace, increasing market share by 35 percent and 130 percent of Melia.

➡

- Established working relations with the golf course and spa. Served as management company point person in the sale of the resort. Installed new back office, front office, and payroll systems. Directed all new collateral and marketing direction of the resort.

- Oversaw the operation of this major resort on the island of St. Thomas. Sapphire Beach has 171 condo suites and a 67-slip condo marina. Was named to 50 Tropical Resorts by *Condé-Nast Traveler* in 1993 and 1994.

- Handled all aspects of operation, development, personnel, and government relations. The resort ran 120 percent of its Market Share and RevPar against the competition, which included Ritz Carlton, Hyatt, Marriott, and Renaissance. Previously served as Vice President/General Manager for Bayside Resorts, responsible for both Sapphire Beach and the 114-condo suite Point Pleasant Resort. Ran both condo associations for both resorts.

Hospitality: Restaurant

Career Summary

General Manager: accomplished Hotel Executive with 20 years experience in food service field; hold distinguished FMP credential.

Manage all areas of the restaurant, including human resources, operations, and marketing, while ensuring that the company's standards of quality and service are maintained.

Maintain an accurate and up-to-date manpower plan of restaurant staffing needs. Prepare management schedules and ensure that the restaurant is staffed for all shifts.

Staffed, trained, and developed restaurant managers and hourly employees through orientations, ongoing feedback, establishing performance expectations, and by conducting performance reviews.

Directly supervised 125 employees.

Knowledge with both NCR and Micros pos systems. Handled purchasing, receiving, and storing food products, inspection of local suppliers, using correct products and proper par levels to minimize food waste and optimize food cost.

Perfect Phrases

- Drove overall in-room dining and honor bar department in Gallup score from number 14 in chain to number five.
- Team leader recipient of Malcolm Baldrige award for quality standards.
- Achievements: Five-Star Employee award winner.
- History of rapid advancement/promotion.
- Raised over $12,000 to benefit local charities by producing and directing musical variety shows.

- First freshman student to be elected Associate Production Director of college television studio.
- Assisted in restructuring and converting the Banquet Department to a self-directed model, assumed managerial duties, and achieved substantial cost savings for the hotel. Reported directly to the Food & Beverage Director.
- Facilitated implementation and continued effectiveness of self-directed work teams.
- Demonstrated proficiency in identifying problem areas, and resolved them in accordance with the Ritz-Carlton nine-step process.
- Participated in a staff compensation task force to benchmark and maximize benefits for the company and employees.
- Managed operational details of various functions, making certain all contractual obligations were fulfilled. Supervised up to 60 employees and ensured that service standards were met. Hired and trained new employees. Assisted with payroll procedures. Produced financial spreadsheets detailing daily revenue for the Banquet Department.
- Highly motivated and results-oriented professional with exceptional leadership and communication skills. Well-rounded restaurant manager with eight years experience in leading and motivating employees and associates in achieving company goals and objectives. Verifiable results of high performance.
- Experienced in positions of Assistant General Manager, Service Manager, Kitchen Manager, and Bar Manager. Dedicated to customer service with a passion to teach and consistently achieve company objectives. Exceptional skills in multitasking and able to identify problems and apply creative solutions for positive outcomes.

➡️

- Responsible for managing 100-plus employees in a $4.6 million high-volume, franchised, full-service worldwide leader in the casual themed dining restaurant.
- Main role and responsibility as Service Manager: recruitment and retention, training, scheduling, personnel reviews, customer service, marketing, and overall operations. Directly responsible for controllable costs as well as COGS. Developed and wrote updated training manuals and developed Friday's "Training Coach" program.
- Oversee restaurant operation with annual sales of $1.5 to $2 million.
- Responsible for the management and operation of multibrand restaurant, including the development and growth of people, sales, and profits.
- Manage operations, including scheduling, daily decision making, delegating tasks, staff support, and guest interaction, while upholding standards, product quality, and cleanliness.
- Monthly financial analysis to evaluate the financial position and to clearly communicate expectations and actions to maximize the restaurant's financial performance.
- Responsible for the restaurant's profit and loss centers, including food, supply, and labor costs to meet the annual operating budget.

Human Resources and Training Professional

Career Summary

Strong HR generalist experience with a proven talent in the development and implementation of training programs for exempt and nonexempt personnel; proven ability to develop material, impart knowledge, and update programs as needed.

Strong research and analytical abilities; notable experience in the management and reduction of costs related to liability and insurance.

Recruiting activities included all aspects of screening, interviewing, hiring, and orientation for union and nonunion staff.

Continuously updated knowledge relevant to workers' compensation, ADA, EEO, Family Medical Leave Act, OSHA, DOT, etc; developed and implemented new procedures to ensure compliance.

Benefits administration experience includes program development, maintenance of costs through negotiations, and the development/implementation of alternative benefit programs.

Assets in collective bargaining activities; successfully administered benefits to assist in successful negotiation.

Generated ongoing bottom-line savings through the introduction of various cost-cutting programs.

Perfect Phrases

- Reduced corporate liability insurance costs by one-third; restructured liability insurance management program to facilitate savings.

- Reduced annual costs by $250K by establishing an effective self-insured plan for supplemental disability.
- Facilitated a one-third reduction in medical benefit costs by implementing an HMO as an integral part of benefits plan.
- Reduced annual paid claims by 45 percent by developing and implementing aggressive claims handling procedures.
- Increased parent company revenues by $185K in six months by reinstituting billing of subsidiary companies for health-care coverage.
- Played an integral role in 12 different collective bargaining agreements—assisted the Senior V.P. by providing benefit guidance.
- Attained a 50 percent conversion from indemnity to managed health care through the creation and implementation of a successful managed care program.
- Facilitated 17 focus groups targeting the executive team, nursing managers, new employees, and experienced employees. The purpose of the focus groups was to gather current state/gap analysis from a selected population who touched the talent acquisition, orientation, and assimilation process.
- Conducted three Process Map Workshops that consisted of hiring managers and HR professionals. The purpose of the one-day workshop was to map out the current state of each process, define gaps, and identify desired state.
- Develop report that identifies all the gaps by process, current cycle time, and best practices with desired cycle time. The goal of the workshop was to prioritize the gaps of the current process and develop a project plan for future work.
- Project Manager leading a large scale recruiting project in the Southeast and Northeast regions. Accountable for

managing the performance of the recruiting and research team, advertising deliverables, and the performance of the technology solution providers. Also responsible for all client communications and for budget review with the stakeholders of the project.

- Conducted an all-day session with HR Directors of Household Consumer Lending Divisions to review the current hiring process, staffing plan, and current metrics.

- Review and evaluation of front-end assessment tools. Developed web-based front-end prescreening tools to immediately identify qualified applicants.

- Developed and managed sourcing strategies for high volume initiative to include virtual job fairs, proactive research, and an on-site job fair in multiple locations.

- Conducted weekly review meetings with the Sales Director within each region to review advertising metrics, number of interviews, number of hires, and quality metrics. Developed a final report for the V.P. of Human Resources that outlined a process map of the current recruiting process, current metrics, and future state recommendations.

- Through the optimization of technology and research, we were able to reduce the cycle time by 30 days and increase the candidate's presented/to hire by 80 percent. We also provided a comprehensive report that provided the organization with technology solutions, process redesign recommendations, program design recommendations, recruiting metrics, and a project plan to help them optimize their talent acquisition process.

- Developed current state map and conducted a second meeting with the team to review gaps, metrics, and desired state models.

- Reviewed current sourcing strategies and negotiated contracts with vendors to increase the traffic/awareness of their current openings.
- Developed RFP to review vendors that could automate front-end process (i.e., applicant tracking systems, automated prescreening tools, and relationship tools that automatically contacted qualified applicants).
- Conducted one-on-one meetings with the Executive Team and Hiring Managers to map out the current state of their recruiting processes.
- Developed front-end reports to track metrics, cycle time, and quality of applicants.
- Developed prescreening tools for hiring managers to use to evaluate candidates during the interview process.
- Conducted an organizational assessment to evaluate how to structure and align the newly created Human Resource Effectiveness Practice to deliver services to the customer.
- Developed an operating plan that defined the purpose of the HR business, all the inputs/outputs of each delivery unit.
- Developed role profiles of the key leadership roles within HR, and hired the leadership team for the newly created Human Resource Effectiveness Practice.
- Conducted a review of the current reward systems and staffing plans for this newly created business.
- Hired a total of 45 senior level candidates to include the Chief Knowledge Officer, Products and Services Leaders for the HR Delivery business, and Senior Consultants within the Research, Measurement, and Communication Practice.
- Conducted interviews with the sales management team to define both the current and desired state.

➡

- Conducted a review of the current technology provider to determine if they have the tools to move the sales organization to self-directed recruiting model.
- Evaluated current third party search firms and selected the top five performers, negotiated contracts, established performance criteria.
- Conducted a review of their current cost per hire, and worked with Corporate Human Resources to purchase corporate contracts for major posting boards to leverage the cost across the business.
- Created requirements documents for 18 pension plans.
- Conducted and facilitated all meetings to define and develop the event flows for all of the pension plans.
- Developed all the event flow templates, and worked with technology to automate the event flows.
- Worked with technology team to automate all the pension calculations.
- Trained participant services representatives on the plans, event flows, and pension calculations in order for them to effectively service the Chrysler account.
- Managed the tasks and the performance of the project team to ensure that deliverable dates were met in order to outsource all aspects of pension administration within a 12-month period.
- Hired 90 sales professionals in a four-month period in order to launch a new sales initiative.
- Developed all the compensation and benefit programs for this newly created joint venture.
- Managed the benefit liabilities and pension liabilities, "and had a dotted line reporting structure directly into the CEO.

Insurance Sales Professional

Career Summary

BSBA/Financial Planning, insurance, and investment sales. Increased customer base, pioneered efforts in new territories. Innovative in Marketing. Multimillion-dollar producer.

Thirteen-year track record for success in networking and selling: number one Sales Rep consistently. Eight years in insurance, five in retail merchandising/distribution.

Took initiative in self-marketing and self-promotion. Developed promotional materials, grew territories by up to 45 percent, achieved a 100 percent client retention rate, and generated strong referral networks.

Capably positioned the companies represented as a preferred provider through extensive personal contact and a mutual respect for clients' time.

Special knowledge and continuing education in investments, retirement and estate planning, securities, mutual funds, annuities, and life and health insurance.

Five-year entrepreneurial background provides a "whatever it takes" commitment to mutual success. Created winning campaigns that boosted sales an average of 22 percent annually. Controlled expenses, motivated staff, and negotiated competitive terms saving 35 percent.

Perfect Phrases

- Successfully convert new investors into educated clients through persistence, patience, empathetic listening, and establishing trust. Added $17 million in new business.

Create and secure leads in the most productive, cost-effective means possible.

- Initially acquired clients exclusively through cold-calling. Achieved increased productivity by hiring outside telemarketers. Warm-call qualified individuals, coordinate appointments, and ask for their business.
- Landed 600-plus new accounts throughout the Texas and Oklahoma region over a four-year period, representing more than $12 million in new business.
- Realize a 98 percent client retention rate—by keeping in touch via personal contact and a self-developed newsletter discussing investment tips, generating increased networking opportunities, a more educated clientele, and better quality attention to their priorities.
- Market annuities, securities, mutual funds, estate planning and personal retirement services, and life and health insurance to personal and corporate investors.
- Through interactive conversation, identify clients' long- and short-term needs. Stress alternatives in their best interest—in one instance saved an investor over $110K in inheritance taxes.
- Recognized for outstanding performance. Sales Agent of the Month 15 times over a three-year period. Sales Agent of the Year in 1996 and 1997. Won various in-house contests.
- Completing Best Insurance Company's Advanced Life Curriculum Program as well as Part 2, Business Life Insurance, of the Life Underwriting Training Council to receive her LUTCF designation.
- Key Accomplishments:

  Millionaire Club 1994; 93 paid apps, $25,447 paid premium

➡

Monthly Activity Average = 65 total apps (30 auto, 15 fire, 10 life, 10 health)

- Took initiative and developed promotional materials, grew territories by up to 45 percent, achieved a 100 percent client retention rate and generated strong referral networks.
- Capably positioned the companies represented as a preferred provider through extensive personal contact and a mutual respect for clients' time.
- Special knowledge and continuing education in investments, retirement and estate planning, securities, mutual funds, annuities, and life and health insurance.
- Five-year entrepreneurial background provides a "whatever it takes" commitment to mutual success. Created winning campaigns that boosted sales an average of 22 percent annually. Controlled expenses, motivated staff, and negotiated competitive terms saving 35 percent.
- Generated $1.5 million in new business within a 22-month period. Prospected new customers via targeted direct mailings. Became involved in local events via memberships with various community organizations.
- Stepped into a nine-county, two-state territory and aggressively pursued leads. Added 200 new accounts, earned membership into "Peak Achiever's Club" in 1991 and 1992.
- Using continued mailings and follow-up surveys, acquired better qualified leads: closed eight out of 10 calls. Number one representative of 24.

IT Professional

Career Summary

Systems Design /Product Engineer.

Strategic Business Planning/Senior-Level Project Management.

Expert in the design, development, and delivery of cost-effective, high-performance technology solutions to meet challenging business demands for well-recognized international corporations including Motorola and Hewlett Packard. Extensive qualifications in all facets of project lifecycle development—from initial feasibility analysis and conceptual design through documentation, implementation, and user training/enhancement.

Equally effective organizational leadership, team building, and project management experience—introducing out-of-the-box thinking and problem-solving analysis to improve processes, systems, and methodologies currently in place to exceed business goals and to perpetually delight shareholders and customers.

Areas of Strength:

National and international marketing
Business research and analysis skills
Strategy identification and implementation skills
Personnel training, team-building, and supervision
Customer service and retention management
Supply chain management
Cost reduction methodologies
Presentation and public speaking skills

Finance management/project budgeting
Quality control management

Computer/Technology
Excel, Word, PowerPoint. Programming languages including Basic, Assembly, C. Use of Unix-Based PC or Macintosh platforms. RF, Wireless, Microcontroller/Microprocessor system skills. Digital and Analog hardware experience. IC design tools: VHDL, Spice, Cadence, Synopsis. Knowledge of technology required to implement small, Portable, battery-powered, wireless multimedia, consumer products into the future.

Perfect Phrases
- Identify technology to meet future needs in the areas of wireless communication products for CTSO division (Core Technologies Systems Organization).
- Work closely with market visionaries to identify future product features—especially those needed for future system integration to be used as a driving force for early technology identification.
- Provide strategic insights—marketing, operational, and product development/enhancement—in making recommendations on what business we should do, with whom, for how long, and why to meet business objectives (time to market, features, and related costs).
- Vendor liaison, i.e., seeking out needed technology, reviewing technology road maps, and managing the nondisclosure agreements for the division, projecting base cost of all semiconductor chips to be designed.
- Memory statistics and benchmarking of embedded/external NVM, ROM, and RAM in relative cost

die area consumption, relative cost trends over time, and cost trend for various memory sizes.

■ Responsible for implementing cost reduction methodologies to reduce direct material cost without adversely affecting manufacturing cost through understanding the supply chain for each technology.

■ Perform analysis of different system approaches to meet market needs, i.e., time to market, features, and costs.

■ Received professional recognition as an "Intersector and International Resource."

■ Changed way of thinking as an option, not previously explored, to meet market needs that are a cost analysis of outsourcing versus traditional in-house methods. This set a precedent that is being used more and more as a strategy to meet business goals and objectives.

■ Program management skills including product feasibility study, specification and contract development, scheduling project tasks, managing outsourcing activity (including legal implications), advertising, and customer support.

■ Digital and analog design simulation; system level simulation and verification; interfacing with layout design personnel; and evaluation/debugging of integrated circuit.

■ Provide technical support to customers to enable the implementation of power management and device driver integrated circuits.

■ Provide documentation/transfer design to outsourcing company for continued manufacturing and technical support.

■ Motley Rice LLC is one of the largest plaintiffs' law firms in the nation. We currently have more than 100,000 active cases, including clients suffering from asbestos and lead

➡

paint exposure, nursing home abuse complications from use of pharmaceutical drugs, aviation safety, and our representation of the 9/11 families.

- Development and implementation of the firm's first IT strategic plan. Negotiation of new local telephone service, cell phone service, and copy/print maintenance contracts saving the firm nearly $200,000 a year.
- Network and server stabilization with the installation of new Cisco switches and routers.
- Enhanced data storage capacity, reliability, and speed of backup with the installation of a Compaq SAN.
- Improved security through the installation of a Cisco firewall, implementation of network translation table and DMZ for our web server and Internet e-mail gateway.
- Standardization on Windows 2000 at the server level and on the desktop.
- Migration from GroupWise to Outlook (accomplished without major problem by in-house staff).
- Migration from WordPerfect to MS Word, and the installation of appropriate firewall and DMZ measures to help secure our network from intrusion.
- Development of the software to gather data from thousands of pages of documentation, and integration of that data with an automated link analysis tool to trace the funding of the 9/11 hijackers.
- Design and development of the firm's five web sites, the firm's intranet, and a secure extranet for collaboration with co-counsel.
- Managed network operations staff responsible for operation of our 40-plus Compaq and HP Blade servers running Windows 2000, MS Exchange, and SQL 2000. We

➥

also have a Compaq Storage Area Network (SAN) with a capacity of 12 terabytes; Compaq tape backup tower is used for daily and weekly backups.

- Implementation of a Cisco-based virtual private network (VPN); and conversion of our major system-case management to a Java/SQL 2000 based solution to track and manage the 100,000-plus cases handled by the firm.
- Development of the company's first information technology strategic plan. Paramount in this effort was the identification of the business needs of the company, current problems, or issues associated with using existing automated solutions and joint development (IT staff working with the business areas) of technology solutions to address those problems.
- Procurement of a state-of-the-market telephone system for our Atlanta call center.
- Conversion of existing MS Access based applications to webcentric environment using Oracle 8i, ASP, and Active X documents.
- Implementation of Cisco's Secure Virtual Private Network solution to replace long distance data lines used to provide remote connectivity to the company's servers; and collaboration with the Chief Medical Officer and epidemiologists to develop software used for medical record abstraction and data quality analysis.
- Recruited to provide leadership to and improve the quality of service provided by the 42-member IT group.
- Reduced salary expense 22 percent, data communications 15 percent, and operating costs 20 percent in first 90 days.
- Initiated server consolidation project to reduce server count by 60 percent while reducing cost and improving

performance and reliability utilizing virtualization technologies.

- Launched an initiative to reduce the number of software tools in use by development and operations.
- Reorganized department to improve service delivery, customer service, and quality assurance.
- Restructured Project Office (PMO) to improve governance.
- Implemented new help-desk service system and quality assurance tools.
- Documented processes and procedures and implemented staffing and procedural changes to ensure compliance with SOX 404 (Sarbanes-Oxley).

Career Summary

At Smith and Woods, achieved a 1,200 percent reduction in line order cuts, exceeded objectives for inventory turns, and reduced total inventory by 15 percent.

Spearheaded production planning, component ordering, and coordination of start-up with co-packers for seven new products.

Minimized scrap losses through disposition of on-hand inventory during formulation and packaging changes, and sales of inventories to contractors.

At TI North America, identified and recovered $1.2 million in supplier overcharges through the development of computer models.

Saved over $500,000 through price renegotiations with vendors.

Devised and maintained cost file spreadsheets by utilizing Bills of Material and costs to determine overall case cost of each product.

Served as team member of Cross-Training Program, Supply Chain Management Team, and numerous task forces.

Perfect Phrases

- Recruited to a high profile position accountable for master scheduling and production planning for 11 co-packers (subcontractors) at 14 locations nationwide for a major consumer products company.
- Managed $1.5 million monthly projected inventory balances for finished goods inventory; ensured attainment of corporate inventory goals and objectives.

➡

- Accountable for 80-plus SKUs and 20-plus different product types, including powders and liquids. Actively participated in new project management. Utilized AMAPS and MPS II computer systems in daily operations.
- Achieved fast-track promotions in recognition of superior performance. Accountable for the development of contract manufacturing supplier strategies for a company specializing in automotive aftermarket products; managed vendor sourcing, price negotiations, packaging development, and internal coordination.
- Supervised material valued at $80 million; held purchase order signature authority to $20,000 and invoice approval authority to $100,000.
- Procured $6 million annually in products and services. Monitored contractor/supplier performance against strategy plans and implemented corrective action. Controlled raw materials and finished goods inventory at subcontractor locations.
- At Reckitt & Colman, achieved a 1,200 percent reduction in line order cuts, exceeded objectives for inventory turns, and reduced total inventory by 15 percent.
- Spearheaded production planning, component ordering, and coordination of start-up with co-packers for seven new products.
- Minimized scrap losses through disposition of on-hand inventory during formulation and packaging changes, and sales of inventories to contractors.
- At Castrol North America Automotive, identified and recovered $1.2 million in supplier overcharges through the development of computer models.
- Saved over $500,000 through price renegotiations with

➡

vendors. Devised and maintained cost file spreadsheets by utilizing Bills of Material and costs to determine overall case cost of each product.

- Served as team member of Cross-Training Program, Supply Chain Management Team, and numerous task forces.
- Change management, lean thinking, strategic and operations planning, and training diverse nonunion and unionized workforces.
- Proficient with several ISO Standards, including the new ISO 9000-2000, MIL-I-45208, ANSI, and ASTM standards.
- Manufacturing experience in a complex plant environment, including sales and customer service leadership roles. Process improvement expertise.
- Complete P&L responsibility for $43M revenue factory (50-plus nonunion employees).
- Reengineered entire factory of recently acquired division.
- Hired entire new staff following acquisition.
- Reduced force by 50 percent while maintaining same output.
- Established companywide quality policy and SPC requirements.
- Prepared plant for customer audits and ISO 9000 certification.
- Purchased line of CNC equipment for high-speed manufacturing. Implemented lean manufacturing practices.
- Full Profit and Loss responsibility for 244-plus associates.
- Reduced inventory over 47 percent, from $2.65MM to $1.4MM, within first five months.
- Increased on-time shipping to better than 98.5 percent to customer requests.

➡

- Designed new shipping configurations, saving company over $1MM annually.
- Diminished headcount over 18 percent, from 244-plus down to 204, saving over $1.4MM per year.
- Consolidated two separate outsourced suppliers and brought production in-house, saving over $3MM.
- Increased productivity over 30 percent, from $16MM sets to over $21MM sets in one year.
- Recruited to turn around 300-employee aluminum wheel manufacturing facility that generates $78 million annually, but has lost $4 million YTD as of August 2005. Hold functional responsibility over human resources, finance, process and manufacturing engineering, new product launch team, operations, safety, quality assurance, materials/purchasing group, and plant engineering/maintenance. Employed lean manufacturing techniques and maintained mandated certifications, including ISO 14001 and Ford Q1.
- Achieved $360,000 in annual savings by eliminating outside contractor inspection operation and instituting upstream quality improvement actions at defect source. Attained 11 percent wheel unit cost improvement within two months as a result, and by optimizing machining bottleneck performance via cycle time, scheduling, and spare parts optimization.
- On target for 22 percent increase in plant capacity through $2.2 million capital program focusing on automating machining operations and robot cell optimization.
- Currently structuring and negotiating $1 million-plus annual contract for machining technical support. New program will serve as model for wheel plants throughout company.

- Reduced scrap rate 21 percent in October 2004 with changes to paint/clear coat line and deburr process.
- Presently overhauling employee recognition programs to more closely match deliverables and enhance communications.
- Turned around poorly performing plant and improved plant efficiency from 78 to 91 percent. Introduced lean manufacturing techniques and led plantwide implementation of Six Sigma, Five S, Kanban, TPM, Kaizen, and SMED, and replaced MRP II system with SAP software.
- Drove plant cost position from sixteenth to sixth and slashed costs $3.12 million annually through a number of initiatives, including labor reduction, washer/ink/spray usage reduction, efficiency gains, spoilage improvement, PM program, and eliminating spending waste.
- Garnered labor savings of $400,000 annually by reducing both salaried and hourly positions by eliminating duplicate tasks, instituting cross training, and combining positions.
- Improved internal spoilage rate by 28 percent while reducing customer complaints 21 percent over three-year period, leading to $216,000 in annual scrap savings.
- Cut workmen's compensation expense by $104,000 annually due to accident free environment.
- Reduced annual logistics and overtime costs $189,000 and overtime, respectively, by eliminating customer assistance from sister plants.
- Completed advanced management program, focusing on international and domestic business strategy.

Career Summaries

Professional Profile

Management professional attuned to the ever-changing needs of business. Extremely service-oriented, with a unique combination of intuitive and analytical abilities. Astute in identifying market plan needs, creating actionable programs, and effectively interacting with the sales field.

Segmentation Targeting	Branding
Financial Forecasting	Advertising
Retail Sales	Sales Promotion
Collateral, Displays and	New Product Rollout
Total Communications Strategist	Strategic Planning

E-Marketing/Online Marketing Director

Award-winning pioneer and expert in web/Internet/new media marketing.

Career profile	Web-savvy marketing professional accomplished in creating and leading high-impact marketing campaigns that consistently meet aggressive e-business goals. Initiated groundbreaking programs and delivered large revenue gains. Excel in both start-up and mature corporate environments. Strong leader known for tenacity and positive "can-do" attitude. Fully fluent in interactive and Internet technologies and tools.
Areas of expertise	■ Web, print, and broadcast advertising ■ Business development initiatives

➡

- Community building and customer loyalty
- E-business strategies and technologies
- Product launch strategy and execution
- Partnership and alliance building
- Online relationship marketing
- Market awareness building
- User acquisition and retention
- Staff development and leadership

Perfect Phrases

- Expert in creating predictive models, customer data mining, consumer pattern recognition, target list segmentation, letter shop and campaign processes, and analytics. Wrote hundreds of proprietary SQL algorithms and targeting models to segment markets and make decisions on what customers will buy and when will they buy it.
- Expert in developing direct marketing plans to meet gross sales and profit targets, including marketing program recommendations, budgeting, unit forecasting, and program ROI analysis. Experienced in modifying marketing plans based on availability of resources and opportunities to maximize ROI on existing marketing programs.
- Strategic and creative marketing and management executive with strong record of contributions in marketing, advertising, and management of people, services, and production. History of effective interaction and relationship management with clients, sales professionals, creative agencies, and multifunctional project teams.
- Expert in driving a cross-functional team (Direct Marketing, Business Management, Sales and Service, Operations and

➡

Fulfillment, Web Commerce Group, etc.) to leverage infrastructure and processes required to successfully execute end-to-end operational implementation of direct marketing programs and retail marketing strategies.

■ Areas of Expertise:

    Marketing campaign design
    Brand recognition
    Special event planning
    Creative content development
    Presentations
    Multimedia production
    Public relations
    New business development
    Project management
    Graphic design
    Copywriting
    Business processes
    Contract negotiations
    Budget development
    Live event production

■ Creation of marketing materials, including: direct mail, brochures, newsletters, sell sheets, advertising print design, ad copy, radio copy, and press releases. Script writing and producing and directing broadcast television segments. Designing content for corporate web sites.

■ Responsible for developing marketing strategies and creative content production, managing a small staff and outside vendors for this full-service marketing consultancy offering specialized services to corporations, as well as small, home-based, and newly created companies.

➡

- Vertically integrated into large organizations, and acted as outside creative communications resource for small companies and agencies to provide a vast array of advertising, marketing, and event planning services.
- Managed the successful implementation of nationwide branding campaign, conferences, and fund-raising events for the Hispanic Scholarship Fund organization. Developed corporate events for BellSouth, Marriott, Mindspring, Pepsi, and Medtrade.
- Led development and execution of marketing strategies and new business initiatives that drove rapid growth from the ground floor to $8.2 million.
- Pioneered a fully functional marketing department infrastructure, including policies and procedures, streamlined business processes, and a talented marketing and communications team.
- Created and deployed unique advertising campaigns proven successful in positioning the company with a competitive distinction. Won national attention for innovative and edgy ads that piqued interest in the target markets.
- Delivered 54 percent ROI from marketing efforts by employing a shrewd balance of Internet and traditional print and broadcast medias to maximize results.
- Negotiated and structured eight major business partnerships and alliances; built and led successful win-win programs through cost-effective co-marketing initiatives.
- Conducted research and initiated new product line in paper products, including product specification development, segmentation identification, and rollout plan. New line gained a 32 percent share within six

months, nearly the P&G average for toiletry products.

- Identified and developed new distribution channel for P&G paper products line, which included retail recruitment, rollout schedule, inventory management, and training schedule. New channel represented a 7 percent share of distribution mix within two years.

- Recommended shift in brand image to target younger buyers, which was successfully implemented and improved name awareness with that segment by 12 percent. Overall brand awareness for individual product lines reached 93 percent in 1997.

- Dedicated extensive time and energy to improving communications with personnel, accepting full responsibility for scheduling, performance reviews, employee motivation, and boosting morale. ESS feedback for our group was in the top 20 percent in all of P&G.

Career Summary

Professional Profile

Thirteen years with Independence Blue Cross, 12 years as departmental supervisor of 12 to 21 registered nurses in care management and coordination.

Seventeen years staff nursing at Columbia Hospital, a leading research and teaching hospital.

Seven years as the quality assurance representative for the ambulatory surgery unit.

Two years case management and cost containment analysis with a home health care provider.

Three years of charge nurse experience at prominent nursing and rehabilitation center.

Perfect Phrases

- Licenses/Certifications:

   Santa Clara County certified as "5150 Evaluator" (72-hour holds for Psychiatric Evaluation)

   IV/Central Line/Blood Withdrawal certificates and experience

   Nationally Registered Emergency Medical Technician (10 years)

   Certified ICU/CCU monitor and EKG technician

   American Heart Association and American Red Cross Instructor certifications

   Certified Patient Care Manager (Hospice)

   ➡

Direct patient care in HIV/AIDS; end-stage. Services included 24-hour availability and care. Counseling for patients and families, medications and treatments, intervention with Emergency Services to minimize stress on patients and families. Care: direct bedside, hands-on; teaching families and loved ones how to care for patient without exposing themselves, through death care and after care. Care always included both nursing and counseling services.

- Teaching Experience:

    CPR Instructor for American Heart Association (1988 to 2001).

    Instructor for American Red Cross (1985 to 1991).

    Taught CPR (Infant, Child, Adult, Community, and Professional Rescuer), First Aid, Advanced First Aid, and Basic Aid Training. Certified in Advanced Life Saving (Lifeguard) for three years. Received five-year service pin & award.

    Mission College Teaching Assistant/Tutor (1989 to 1990).

    Tutoring/Assistant Teaching in Pharmacology, Mathematics for Medications, Anatomy and Physiology, and other science courses for the Mission College Psychiatric Technician Program, under the supervision of Margaret Boone, RN, PHN, MA; approved by the Board(s) of Nursing.

- Nursing professional with over 30 years of experience in Facility Site/Medical Record Audits, Delegation Oversight, Utilization Review, MCQA, NIPAC, Tile XXII, OBRA, OSHA, ➡

and JACHO. Extensive experiences with organizational skills and self-motivation, management skills, director of nursing skills, and 15 years clinical experience (ICU, ER, BURN UNIT, Medical and Ortho).

- Registered Nurse: recent RN grad with recent but intense practical experience in hospital (ICCU/ACCU) and primary care environments. Day-to-day management of high acuity patients on Medication/Surgery. ICCU computer-skilled, managing heavy daily patient volume.

- Proficient in all documentation/record maintenance/paperwork to ensure accuracy and patient confidentiality.

- Exceptional grasp of managed care: excellent mastery of supervisory skills and demonstrated leadership in supervising, training, and auditing Registered Nurses conducting case management and discharge planning at several HCA hospitals. In-depth knowledge of health benefit programs: coverage requirements, medical and departmental policy, procedures, practice, terminology, and pharmaceuticals. An active participant in numerous care management and coordination departmental initiatives.

- Achievements include developing the Independence Blue Cross On-site Review Program and generating and maintaining positive and communicative relations at several challenging health-care facilities.

- Highly proficient in contributing to and reaching team solutions, generating and maintaining positive relations with internal and external clients, maintaining all compliance standards, working well under pressure, and producing error-free work of high quality.

- Credentials:

➡

Board Examination 01/2005

License, State of Texas 07/2004

ICCU/ACCU Staff Nurse, Good Samaritan Hospital, Suffern, New York, Medical Office/Nurse

- Medical Office Skills: scheduling clients, taking vital signs and initial assessments, scheduling tests, calling in prescriptions, taking phone calls from patients and other physicians, setting up exam rooms, assisting physician with exams, pap smear, flexible sigmoidoscopy, 12-lead EKG, cleaning, and autoclaving equipment.
- Clerical Skills: Answering phones, filing, ordering supplies, daily reports, money handling and scheduling; Microsoft Office, MS Windows, keyboarding, 10-key, e-mail, Internet.
- Customer Service Experience: Customer complaints and problem solving.
- Chief Nurse of a large ambulatory clinic serving over 50,000 clients in a federally funded setting. Oversaw three large clinics with 20 nursing personnel. Responsible for scheduling, recruiting, evaluating, budgeting, ordering, and monitoring all clinic operations with 11 Family Practice physicians.
- Chairman of the Patient Focus Committee, Infection Control Committee, and Performance Improvement Committee. Commended for bringing many clinic improvements.
- Interim Director of Nursing: directed the nursing activities in multispecialty Ambulatory Surgery Center (ASC) consisting of three Operating Rooms, a seven bed Recovery Room, an Endoscopy Lab, and a Fertility Clinic.

➡

- Managed all nursing activities to include major equipment acquisition worth more than a million dollars, policy development, scheduling, accreditation preparation, quality improvement and utilization management, marketing, budgeting, and supervision of 26 personnel. Commended for problem solving and developing over 230 policies and procedures.
- Current Licenses/Certifications:

    Registered Nurse

    Licensed Psychiatric Technician

    American Heart Association, CPR/BCLS (AED)

    CPI (Crisis Prevention/Intervention) Certified

    Certified Director of Staff Development (DSD)

Paralegal

Career Summaries

A results-oriented Legal Assistant experienced in legal administration and paralegal studies involving research, writing, investigation, litigation support, mediation/arbitration techniques, rules of evidence, and dissolution of marriage proceedings. Familiar with word processing, spreadsheet, docket control, and database applications. Key responsibilities included:

> Drafted and filed motions, interrogatories, initial and responsive pleadings.
>
> Tracked client employment records and other information using various sources.
>
> Helped clients fill out income, expenses, and property statements.
>
> Prepared settlement agreements and other closing documents.

Nearly seven years experience in a law firm with general practice cases, including bankruptcy, criminal, family law, civil litigation, business setup, and estate administration.

Successfully settled numerous collection, countersuit, bankruptcy, and preference cases and claims.

Member and chairperson of two (state) creditor committees that assisted in recovery of millions of dollars of unsecured claims for various creditors.

Created database on Microsoft Access of open and closed files with cross-reference of names of principals associated with files.

Recovered over $1 million in bad debt recovery for company.

Perfect Phrases

- Litigation paralegal/legal secretary: conduct legal research; draft, summarize, and/or transcribe documents and correspondence—pleadings, discovery, trial preparation; calendar; schedule; arrange travel.

- Insurance claims/legal background: 11 years staff counsel experience; insurance courses completed: risk management, claims, operations, financial/statutory accounting and regulations, business and financial analysis, legal environment, commercial/personal property risk, and liability management.

- Litigation legal assistant to partner in law firm. Drafted, summarized, and transcribed records, correspondence, pleadings, and discovery (provided legal research and writing of memos, points, and authorities and declarations); managed litigation process, heavy client contact (including investigation and responses to discovery), and coordination of international travel.

- Responsible for running a staff counsel office separate from the insurance company's Branch and Home Office. Administered, updated, and repaired LAN/WAN (local and wide area network) with telephone help from Home Office. Administered accounts payable/receivable for office, and prepared accountability reports of same to Home Office.

- Provided litigation support to managing attorney, including document management, legal research, drafting, summarizing or transcribing of documents; heavy client and claims department contact; calendaring coordination.

- Full-time litigation secretary and legal assistant for an AV rated law firm.

➡

- Competent in legal writing, scheduling motion calendars, special set hearings, and client interaction etiquette.

   Diligent in keeping deadlines, scheduling, and billing.

   Experienced in the procedures of the Circuit Court (civil and family divisions) and the District Court of Appeals.

   Able to give assistance in preparing for depositions, hearings, vetting witnesses, expert witnesses, and trial preparation.

   Knowledge of the [state] Rules of Court and the procedures required in civil procedures.

- Substantive legal work in a paralegal/legal assistant position. Responsible for initial meetings with clients for intake of information and case analysis.

   Manage cases to meet deadlines and provide client support.

   Draft pleadings and correspondence.

   Prepare pleadings for filing with the court.

   Organize discovery responses and prepare for submitting to opposing attorney.

   Coordinate and monitor attorney's personal calendar and docket schedule.

   Prepare bankruptcy petitions and file via electronic case filing system.

   Discuss preliminary and postbankruptcy issues with clients.

   Experienced with lift stay motions, consent orders, and other bankruptcy court motions.

➡

- Prepare all estate planning documents, and assist clients with funding of Revocable Trust Agreements. Assist attorney with the formation of corporations and limited liability companies, also assist in filing domestic and civil complaints. Administrative duties include preparing daily deposit for general operating account, posting client payments, and paying the bills for the firm.

Career Summary

Career Profile

National Board for Certification in Occupational Therapy No. 004127.

Texas Board of Occupational Therapy, License No. 019243.

Analysis for all clients in the industrial rehab program.

Identified the Physical, Environmental, Psychophysical, and Psychosocial risk factors for clients employed in industrial and office settings.

Recommended controls for process flow, safety equipment, and ergonomically designed workstations/seating used to reduce risk hazards in industrial and office settings.

Perfect Phrases

- On call for very exclusive, high profile, 150 member-only center for preventative medicine.
- Partnered with staff nutritionists, psychologists, physical therapists, massage therapists, and exercise therapists to provide customized, one-on-one care for clients.
- Able to perform Swedish, deep tissue, sports, and medical massage as well as reflexology and Table Shiatsu.
- Trained in a variety of spa treatments and body wraps.
- Responsible for Work Conditioning, Job Simulation, Job Coaching, and Job Performed VDT Ergonomic Analysis, and facilitated training sessions on Injury Prevention, Posture, Body Mechanics, Joint Protection, and Energy Conservation Techniques to improve Work Efficiency/Productivity and injury reduction.
- Educated clients on the Abnormal Illness Behavior

Cycle and its correlation to Pain Management. Collaborated with Engineering, Safety, and Management to integrate workplace operations, processes, and conditions to reduce the number of low back strain and musculoskeletal injuries with Nursing Staff and Material Handlers.

- Supervise Physical Therapy interns in performing routine activities, and conduct training needs regularly to upgrade the skills required to meet company's quality standard. Motivates and supports the care team; anticipates and overcomes problems that may affect residents care or care staff.

- Delegates' staff to train interns and Junior Physical Therapist for clinical experience and/or observation in their respective areas. Instructs and delegates Physical Therapy interns to formulate home program for patients and their families to continue treatment at home.

- Administers diagnostic tests and physiotherapeutic treatment, such as:

  Assigns and monitors Physical Therapy interns in performing patients' activities of Daily Living, such as ambulation, maintaining personal hygiene, and proper nourishment. Teaches functional employment skills, including proper lifting techniques and functional strength testing.

  Monitors therapeutic exercise to increase endurance, strength, and coordination for specific muscle groups or entire body. Evaluates and trains sitting and standing balance, transfer, and mobility. Progressive gait training, with or without ambulatory aids offered, including instruction in negotiating barriers and obstacles such as rough grounds, ramps, and chairs. ➡

Offers various Physical Therapy modalities such as superficial/deep heat/cold, as well as other hydrotherapy techniques and electrotherapy techniques and massage.

- Managed busy rehabilitation with patients by treating according to the rehab standard.
- Successfully working in all areas of the rehabilitation as required, and treating patient at the highest possible level at all times.
- Advocated and linked chronic mentally ill consumers with needed services.
- Independently provided services in the community. Set independent schedule, including productivity that was consistently 10 to 15 percent above productivity requirement.
- Provided individual and group therapy to chronic mentally ill consumers.
- Monitored medication of mentally ill consumers. Supervised care of chronic mentally ill consumers (psychiatric, medical, and activities of daily living). Minor case management duties as required, paperwork included: daily vouchers, monthly treatment plans, authorization requests, quarterly. Developed therapeutic groups for individuals with varying needs.

Product Management

Career Summary

Professional Profile

Seven years experience in product management for Fortune 75 consumer products company with high brand awareness, and winner of numerous consumer product awards.

Segmentation Targeting	Offer Development
Financial Forecasting	Advertising
Channel Development	Sales Promotion
Collateral, Displays, and Marcom	New Product Rollout
Total Communications Strategist	Strategic Planning

Perfect Phrases

- Led strategic development for new health/beauty property launch, developing market launch plan, aligning multi-functional team to changes in pricing and packaging, and coordinating copy development with advertising agency.
- Won alignment of senior management to pricing changes for new product launch. Proficiency in financial modeling, analysis of consumer preferences, and an open, collaborative approach contributed to a strategic and financially optimal choice.
- Synthesized health and beauty segment data from numerous sources, developing competitive profiles on key competitors. Extensively employed data from IRI, industry analyses and literature, and feedback from sales force and consumer focus groups, among others. Knowledge was employed to inform new product selection, guide market research, and refine product launch plans.

169

- Extensively engaged key functional stakeholders throughout the planning process—sales, market research, finance, packaging, operations, marketing services, legal, and external vendors—to ensure optimal product launch.
- Analyze market requirements, in-house technical strengths, and competitive threats, to develop a strategic product road map of product features for current and future product releases.
- Produce business case, cost, pricing, and competitive analysis reports to upper management to win approval for product development.
- Manage beta tests at selected customer sites to provide support and get feedback on early product versions to improve products and increase customer satisfaction
- Develop product strategy and supervise product direction from concept through obsolescence to produce three new product releases.
- Gather and analyze product requirements and manage development with engineering to meet product release schedules.
- Produce white papers, data sheets, sales training, order forms, and provide sales support for all product releases to enable sales process.
- Develop test plan to determine if all business case requirements had been met, and track user issues through to resolution with engineering.
- Manage cross-functional teams of developers, tech writers, and network engineers to produce fully integrated products.
- Achieved strong and sustainable revenue for the

company through demonstrated knowledge of financial and product management practices. Expertly determined long-range objectives and managed projects within or below established budgets.

- Gather technical requirements, prepare proposals, and manage the implementation of product features with corporate operations, marketing, and sales efforts. Create and monitor business metrics. Analyze revenue streams; establish and manage costs, draft schedules, and product delivery. Keen insight for reviewing processes and advising production and operations.

- Planned and drafted a formal, master production schedule for annual and five-year product manufacturing plans based on current and projected trends.

- Made sales presentations to 40 of the Fortune 100 list of companies, explaining converged network services and how ION represented a new approach to voice and data networking.

- Developed product implementation process for new platform, including training, support of the sales staff, and resolution of issues related to implementation.

- Evaluated key retail clients' product segment strengths and weaknesses; cooperated with key retail clients to develop strategies and guidelines to modify and complement in-process product lineup.

- Negotiated and implemented private label/branded consumer product agreements, guidelines, and contracts with both retail clients and suppliers.

- Developed key channel strategies with major retail clients and formally presented various proposals to both internal and retail clients' decision makers.

➡

- Built cross-functional teams between the marketing, purchasing, material control, and engineering department to quickly resolve product issues, develop new products, reduce procurement costs and efficiency, and provide the quickest production turnaround and shipping time possible for key retail clients.

Career Summaries

Areas of Expertise

Multiunit manager for best-in-class retailer with premium brand awareness and reputation.

Recruiting, training, and developing staff to high performance levels.

Scheduling employees in accordance to customer traffic and demand.

Displaying eye-catching merchandise and planograms to increase impulse purchasing and impact sales.

Reducing costs and shrink to ensure optimum profitability.

Overseeing all functions pertaining to operations, including sales, adherence to company policy, controlling shrinkage, maintaining inventory levels, customer service, and strategic planning.

Career Highlights:

Lowest turnover in region of 11 districts and 145 stores.

Achieved 123 percent of revenue objectives.

Instrumental in the success of seven new store launches.

Slashed budget expenditures by 11.7 percent while gaining enhanced productivity.

Invited as Key Speaker at company's conference in recognition of outstanding performance.

Perfect Phrases

- A multiunit retail sales and operations manager skilled in driving high sales performance, P&L management, strategic planning, and business development in start-up, growth, and contract managed environments.

- P&L responsibility for a 210,000 square foot design center selling design and remodeling services, including 10 specialty showrooms and a trade services office.

- Won the Marcus Award, Home Depot's top award for volunteerism and community involvement.

- Increased project sales penetration to a chain-leading 24 percent and improved service recovery by developing a new customer service matrix.

- As one of 30 managers representing 1,700 store managers to senior management, nominated for and joined the prestigious Home Depot Store Manager Council.

- P&L responsibility for 36 Borders stores in the Southeast. With sales of $219 million, led field management team of District Managers, Area Marketing Managers, Regional Human Resources Manager, and Recruiters.

- Increased market share from 18 to 23 percent and controlled costs during industrywide sales downtrend.

- Increased customer service scores through a focus on a selling culture and implementation of new customer service standards.

- Built and strengthened celebrity relationships and product placement opportunities, creating brand awareness via award shows, movie premieres, press junkets, and movie wardrobing opportunities.

- Opened 10 domestic freestanding stores. Responsible for the daily store press activities, including the Madison

Avenue flagship store opened in summer 2005.

- Responsible for all product, marketing, licensing, and strategic planning activities of private label brands for the Internet, stores, catalog, and new businesses. Merchandise areas include: Toys, Juvenile Home Furnishings, and Accessories.
- Directed the development and implementation of the private label branding strategy on Toysrus.com, which increased sales by 150 percent and improved margin by 30 points.
- Developed Hispanic product and marketing strategy for private label brands. Sales increased 30 percent in Hispanic market areas.
- Expanded the merchandise assortment and circulation of a direct mail Toy Guide for Kids. Sales increased 60 percent.
- Initiated new premium and promotional business for the company to create additional brand exposure, licensing opportunities, and a new revenue stream.
- Achieved annual sales of $600 million.
- Revamped the strategic direction of the catalog media plan, developed new private brand merchandise assortment, and improved return on equity by 20 percent.
- Negotiated and implemented new syndicated media programs to enter totally new merchandise and catalog businesses, which created a multimillion-dollar revenue source.
- Developed Internet programs, which resulted in the three most productive categories in the company.
- Directed all merchandise, marketing, and strategic planning activities in the catalog and Internet merchandising division. Merchandise areas included: Home Furnishings,

➡

Electronics, Sporting Goods, Health/Personal Care, and Toys.

- Established catalog returns reduction task force, which reduced customer returns by 12 percent and improved profits by 20 percent.
- Ensures that staff is informed about changing regulations, and communicates changes to impacted areas of the company.
- Ensures that all compliance activities are properly documented and compliance files are maintained.
- Stabilized troubled location by recruiting, training, and motivating an entirely new team of 40 employees. Promoted and coached 10 employees to become successful in supervisory and management positions.
- Participates and provides leadership in activities in the community to promote the image of the company.
- Audits other store locations to ensure compliance with company's policies, and verifies inventory in stock.
- Opened seven new Wal-Mart Discount/Supercenter stores ranging from 95,000 to 230,000 square feet. Units managed ranged from $2.5 to $105 million in sales volume, inventory range from $1.5 to $8 million. Responsible from empty building to Grand Opening Ceremony in four weeks and three days.
- Managed over 630 Store Associates in one location. Regional Trainer of five states, trained over 550 managers in operations, merchandising, and leadership. Certified Franklin Quest time management Facilitator. Walton Institute of Retailing graduate.
- Walton Food Institute graduate Serve Safe Certified.

Retail Sales Associate

Career Summary

Profile

Enthusiastic sales associate with proven record of achieving challenging goals of the organization. Personable and reliable team player with ability to gain trust and confidence. Improved employee morale by exhibiting cheerful, helpful attitude. Innovative and resourceful, with reputation of adhering to high ethical standards.

Strengths:

Customer Retention	Merchandising
Service Quality	Customer Engagement
Inventory Control	Sales Leadership
Employee Management	Employee Training
Order Processing	

Perfect Phrases

- Number-one ranked salesman for four straight years.

  Excellent at engaging customers and achieving high closing rate.

  Focused on performance management and always conscious of sales targets.

  Strong product knowledge from five years' experience in the field.

- Promoted from Sales Associate to Key Sales Associate.
- Independently opened and closed store, maintained sales records, and performed banking functions and evening deposits. ➡

- Over four years combined retail-selling experience. Over one year creative design experience (painting, jewelry design, interior design). Strengths include good customer contact skills and multiple single customer sales. Enjoy meeting new people. Considered "hardworker" and "great salesman" by employers.
- Highly motivated, creative, and ambitious customer service representative with over five years of experience in the sales industry. Demonstrated expertise in all areas of retail, including marketing, merchandising, and sales. A convincing and credible communicator with customers, coworkers, and senior management. Ability to prioritize multiple projects and adapt to changing environments while working well under pressure. Able to work resourcefully and independently as well as collectively and creatively within a team structure. Outgoing personality enhances all aspects of customer service.
- Sales expertise in all areas of the store, including cosmetics; women's, men's, children's, and juniors clothing; women's shoes; housewares; jewelry; and accessories.
- Enhanced customer service and increased profits by suggestive selling and extensive knowledge of store's products, primarily in women's shoes, women's clothing, and cosmetics.
- Artistic design and marketing of store products by remodeling projects that enhanced the store's appearance.
- Cash balance and handling with register by sales, returns, exchanges, payments, and opening new accounts.
- Responsible for display and sale of designer jewelry, watches, and fine quality diamonds. Achieved sales of over $350,000 in the first year. Opened and closed daily store

➡

operations, balanced receipts, shipped and received merchandise, and performed inventory for two locations.

- Consistently solved problems to customer satisfaction in this fast-paced sales environment.
- Professionally advised customers on the appropriate merchandise to meet their needs.
- Promoted repeat customers by establishing customer rapport and conducting follow-up as needed.
- Assisted store manager with store displays, merchandising, and sales promotions.
- Assisted with the opening of The Silk Trading Co., new concept store in Costa Mesa, California.
- Worked with the store manager with the daily closing report and daily sales report.
- Assisted in scheduling sales associates and determining goals for counter and sales associates. Assisted with initiating and executing special events. Responsible for achieving personal weekly and monthly goals through sales presentations, product knowledge, and promotional activities.

Career Summaries

Sales/Sales Management Executive

Cutting-edge computer and Internet technologies.

Key Account Management ■ New Business Development ■ Direct Sales and Reseller Partnerships

Consultative and Solution Sales ■ Networking and Relationship Building ■ Contract Negotiations

PROFILE Dynamic 14-year sales career reflecting pioneering experience and record-breaking performance in the computer and Internet industries. Remain on the cutting edge, driving new business through key accounts and establishing strategic partnerships and dealer relationships to increase channel revenue.

■ Expert in sophisticated e-commerce sales models, and vast knowledge of both the e-business marketplace and the capabilities and complexities of products.

■ Outstanding success in building and maintaining relationships with key corporate decision makers, establishing large-volume, high-profit accounts with excellent levels of retention and loyalty.

■ Exceptionally well-organized, with a track record that demonstrates self-motivation, creativity, and initiative to achieve both personal and corporate goals.

"Brad is a dynamic leader and arguably one of the best salespeople that has ever worked on any of the

➡

sales teams I have managed. I highly recommend Brad for a position within any organization."
—VP of Sales, Millennium Software

Sales/Marketing/Sales Management

INTERNET BANKING AND FINANCIAL SERVICE INDUSTRIES
Senior Sales and Business Development executive with proven ability to drive business growth through aggressive sales initiatives that deliver revenue growth, market share, and market penetration. Conceptual thinker and strategic planner who balances sales production and sales leadership. Experienced in technology/product launch and market expansion. Well-versed in dealing with diverse operational units (Legal, IS/IT, Finance, HR, Investor Relations).

> Cross-Functional Team Building and Leadership
> Consultative Sales
> Internet Business Development and Implementation
> Contract Terms and Negotiation
> Competitive Analysis and Product Positioning
> Relationship Marketing

Strong background in identifying, establishing, and managing strategic relationships to leverage and generate significant business opportunities. Talented motivator with keen business acumen.

Perfect Phrases

- Top-producing Sales Executive with more than 15 years experience in the development, commercialization, and market launch of leading edge technologies worldwide. Combined expertise in strategic planning, P&L management, marketing, tactical sales, and client relationship management. Outstanding record of achievement in solutions selling and complex contract negotiations. Diverse industry and multichannel sales experience within the financial services, banking, health care, retail, and Fortune 500 market sectors.

- Directed global account team responsible for revenue growth, retention, and service of select group of SBC's largest accounts. Built relationships with multiple levels of each customer organization while positioning team members for focus on defined projects and business needs.
- Received promotion to premier level of account support within SBC after two years of successful account management within large business group.
- Currently manage diverse team of product, technical, and sales support resources with direct reporting responsibilities.
- Successful Account Manager with 13 years of experience and a proven record of increasing revenue and complex product sets while providing the highest level of customer service and integrity. Skilled at developing and maintaining longstanding professional relationships within varied functional units of customers and internal groups.
- Demonstrated success in managing individual teams as well as entire organizations, with responsibilities including customer service, revenue growth, technical support, and policy development.
- High-energy sales professional with over 15 years of "business to business" experience dealing with Fortune 1000 business, government, medical, and telecommuni-

➡

cations markets. Strong team building and management skills and a passion for helping companies achieve success. Excellent technical background in enterprise-level voice, data, and related IT technologies

- Leadership for customer satisfaction, business development, and vendor relationships. Managed to a $26 million quota. Focused on voice, convergence, and contact center solutions from Nortel, Siemens, Cisco, and Ericsson. Currently developing our infrastructure and mobility practice for structured cabling and broadband wireless.
- Achieved 133 percent of branch quota in 2004, President's Club award winner, top four of 124 sales reps.
- Achieved 118 percent of branch quota in FY 2004, President's Club award winner.
- Eleven-plus years proven record of accomplishments within the pharmaceutical industry.

  Ranked first of 94 in the region, first in the district (2005)

  Ranked second of 94 in the region, second in the district (2003)

  Ranked third of 86 in the region, first in the district (2001)

  Six-time President's Club Award Winner (overall); ranked within top 5 percent in overall sales and attainment

  Continuously exceeding quota and Market Share for products being paid on (Zyrtec, Frova)

  Member of District of the Year (2002)

  Exercise initiative and independent judgment to exceed sales quotas

➡

- Global Sales/Alliance Manager to the Hewlett-Packard Company. Primary responsibility is for worldwide field engagement, aligning i2 Account Managers with HP Client Business Managers in i2s and HP's most strategic accounts. Developed and implemented a Proactive Teaming Initiative that got sponsorship from both i2s EVP WW Sales and HP's EVP WW Strategic Accounts.
- Responsible for facilitating executive-level relationships between HP's and i2's "C-Level" executives, as well as ensuring the "technical integrity" of the alliance. Annual quota of not less than $350M attained at 125 percent.
- Senior Sales Manager with $125 million global manufacturer of scarves. Scope of responsibility includes strategic planning, competitive assessment, market positioning, business development, new product introductions, and client relationship management. Direct a team of seven.
- Led the successful national market launch of three product lines. Met first year projections, and currently on track to achieve 15 percent increase for 1998.
- Built and managed key account relationships with major retailers, catalog companies, and specialty stores, including Bergdorfs, Bloomingdale's, Macy's, Neiman Marcus, and Saks.
- Worked with home office in Italy to facilitate the design, test marketing, and U.S. introduction of an upscale private label line. Achieved immediate market penetration, with projections for $25 million in first year revenues.
- Developed strategy to leverage D'Italia's position within nontraditional business sectors. Negotiated contracts with the NCAA Collegiate Licensing Committee and several others.

Sales: Consultative

This section of phrases to support consultative selling is a complement to sales phrases in general. Not all sales positions leverage consultative selling to the same degree. A systems integrator with IBM will leverage this approach more than a pharmaceutical sales person, who in turn will use it more than a retail salesperson.

Perfect Phrases

■ Increased customer sales presentations by 50 percent coaching a consultative selling process.

■ Reliance on consultative sales approach and process improvement recommendations. Managed territory with $13 million yearly revenue stream. Integration of third party hardware, software, and services to enable Xerox print solutions. Developed high-level consultative relationship. Managed the channel sales team for Missouri for two years.

■ Accomplishments:

Increased installed base each year by an average of 28 percent.

Consistently placed in top 5 o 10 percent of approximately 250 nationwide sales reps.

Top ranking among peers of 98 percent in customer retention over nine years.

Achieved President's Club 1991, 1993, 1995, 1996, 1997, and 1999 (160 percent of plan).

■ Developed and delivered first formal sales management training program focused on building competencies in managing a consultative sales force according to group's➡

unique operating model. Completed competency analysis, mapping gaps to drive curriculum.

- Accomplished sales performance expert experienced in marketing and business development. Proven record of success in the design and delivery of training and development programs that drive revenue generation and business results. Skillful strategist with consultative approach. Able to work effectively across organizations to identify needs and build customized training, process, and tool solutions. Valued for ability to identify best practices and integrate them into day-to-day operations. Respected, influential leader known for a company-first approach. Pragmatically focused on value-based selling and business benefit capture.
- Drove integration of consultative selling skills through in-class training that assimilated methodology into sales tools and sales presentations, as well as into sales management curriculum.

Eleven years experience as crew leader for residential construction, rough carpentry.

Directed a crew of 10 people on the job site in one of largest housing developments in Dallas.

Built loyal client base through personal attention, quality service, and consistency.

Established reputation for excellence within local communities.

Demonstrated ability to work efficiently and effectively in fast-paced environment.

Perfect Phrases

- Successfully completed building project that was behind schedule when first hired, saving the company from liquidated damages.
- Daily management of projects and subcontractors to keep projects on schedule to ensure completion on time.
- Owned small local company and performed project planning, scheduling, and estimating for commercial and residential construction projects. Scope of responsibility included interfacing with subcontractors, obtaining permits, ordering materials, reviewing proposals, and liaising between county officials and owners. Supervised several subcontractors, including electricians, plumbers, air-conditioning installers, framers, and concrete finishers.
- Successfully led reconstruction of home that increased property value by $10,000.
- Managed all construction personnel in new construction of large commercial complexes for this small company that provides road construction services to Florida military

bases. Held weekly meetings, ensuring progress of six carpenters, laborers, and concrete finishers in accordance with requirements while maintaining compliance with Occupational Health.

- Energized internal employee efforts that saved company 25 percent in subcontracted labor expenses.
- Expedited storm drain portion of project and reduced labor cost by hiring appropriate skilled subcontractor.
- Tasked with construction of two-story outpatient clinic as on-site supervisor for a large commercial construction company. Communicated with Navy inspectors, resolved job-site problems, reviewed plans and specifications, and ensured timely completion of new construction and renovations of eight floors in hospital.
- Accomplished 35 percent savings by training and leading employees to construct concrete stairways and elevator shafts.
- Led employee completion of all operating rooms, saving 25 percent in potential subcontracted labor expenses.
- Brought on to perform project planning and scheduling for subcontractor crew of framers, plumbers, electricians, and other laborers that completed construction of 262-room student housing building for Michigan State University. Allocated materials and labor as necessary; directed superintendent, assistant superintendent, and field engineer.
- Generated $50,000 revenue savings for company by completing 18, rather than 14, buildings by deadline.
- Reduced labor costs by 25 percent by hiring two Sheetrock companies and instigating competition.
- Chosen by multifamily and student housing construction company to provide project management for three major

➡

projects: four four-story buildings at University of Florida, four apartment buildings at apartment complex in Tennessee, and one three-story building at a Hampton Inn in Oklahoma. Led subcontractors, interfaced with owners and city officials, obtained proper permits, and oversaw assistant superintendent and independent consultants.

- Completed university project within critical time constraints through proactive leadership of punch crew.

- Identified and corrected structural problem at Marriott that saved company time and expense.

- Guided several subcontractors on job site for small company, providing framing and construction of exterior walls for various clients, including Shoney's Inns in Pensacola, Florida, and Houston, Texas. Hired and supervised 22 metal framers and Sheetrock employees, ordered materials, and tracked labor costs within budgetary constraints.

- Accurately ordered and delivered materials, finding the best supplier prices, ensuring that no materials were wasted and achieving consistent cost savings.

- Delegated duties to various subcontractors, completed estimations, monitored materials and equipment on daily basis, and managed supply houses. Interfaced with owners and architects.

- Employed creative techniques when repairing old structures with limited original materials; successfully repaired 100-year old building with 300 damaged bricks, blending new materials with existing structure.

Dedicated educator with 20-plus years of teaching experience. Recognized for innovation in program development, instruction, and administration to meet the needs of a broad range of students. Effective communicator, writer, administrator, and student advisor/advocate.

Core Competencies

Curriculum Development and Instruction:
- Assisted in the development, validation, and enhancement of curricula. Introduced hands-on tools (e.g., computer technology, outside classroom activities) to improve classroom interest and retention.
- Taught a full academic curriculum (e.g., reading, writing, communications, mathematics, social science) to children ages seven to 13.
- Designed and implemented customized teaching programs to allow emotionally, physically, and learning disabled students to be mainstreamed into the classroom.
- Launched a highly successful peer tutoring program designed to improve interaction between upper level and younger students while fostering communication and mentoring skills at all levels.

Administration and Special Activities:
- Appointed Vice Principal with responsibility for a diversity of functions, including faculty recruitment and scheduling, curriculum development, discipline, parent/community affairs, and special events planning.
- Prepared documentation for recertification by the National Accreditation of Schools Committee as a member of a

➡

cross-functional faculty/administration committee.
- Provided classroom training, performance evaluation, and motivation as a mentor to student teachers completing college requirements for an education degree.

Community and Public Relations:
- Built partnerships with local companies and developed a series of seminars to introduce junior high school students to the business world. Coordinated speaker selection and topics of discussion.
- Participated on cross-functional teams of educators and administrators to design programs to improve the quality of educational curricula, enhance parent and community relations, and increase student participation both inside and outside of the classroom.

Perfect Phrases
- Administered curriculum for fifth and sixth grade Special Education students (emotionally disturbed, learning disabled, and neurologically impaired). Developed lesson plans and instructed all major subject areas, including reading, grammar, science, and social studies. Assessed student abilities and evaluated performance; conducted parent-teacher conferences to provide parents with student development reports. Counseled students and parents to resolve learning and discipline problems. Developed monthly newsletters and participated in IEP meetings for each child.
- Taught fourth grade for three years and full day kindergarten for four years. Directed the preschool and junior kindergarten program for one year. Revised curriculum and reading program for kindergarten class. Generated

progress reports and evaluated students through report cards. Authored monthly newsletters. Created lesson plans and developed learning centers. Accountable for kindergarten screening and direction/production of annual holiday pageant.

- Established a class of 20 "overload" kindergarten students three weeks after the beginning of the school year. Supported the curriculum by planning and implementing standards-based lessons using visual cues, movement, and music.
- Modified lessons to serve ELL students and students with various learning styles. Created and maintained relationships and communication with the parents. Taught intervention classes to ELL students before school twice a week. Volunteered for PTA and community projects outside of class hours.
- Provided one-on-one and small group tutoring in basic skills of reading, writing, math, science, and social studies.
- Received the Service to Youth Award by a Nonparent.
- Co-taught two regular eighth grade and one honors Earth Science classes. Planned weekly instruction, developed lesson plans, administered exams, supervised students performing lab activities, graded labs and homework assignments, and recorded grades.
- Taught eighth grade English, stressing creative and critical thinking skills, including instruction in grammar, spelling, vocabulary, and creative and technical writing.
- Developed and wrote lesson plans that followed curriculum guidelines. Instructed students in project development through use of the writing process from topic selection to publication or presentation.

➡

- Taught seventh grade public speaking course focusing on the development and oral presentation of individual ideas.
- Currently employed at a child-care facility. Many years of experience in daily teaching as the owner/operator of a home-based day care.
- Experienced volunteer preschool teacher, youth director, and puppet ministry director at church, with additional experience working with children through other varied volunteer activities.
- Home-schooled three children for several years.
- Hosted Fresh Air child/children (seven summers).
- Red Cross First-Aid and CPR certified.
- Collaborated with city officials to petition for rezoning of a residential area; gained approval to further develop a proposed Children's Nature Trail with varied accommodations for children with special needs.
- Experienced in successfully working with Special Education students and developing skills in students at all levels of achievement.
- Utilize creative skills to design and implement well-received lesson plans and program structure.
- Establish learning environments that meet the physical, emotional, intellectual, social, and creative needs of children.
- Create yearly course work, including the selection of teaching materials.
- Effectively counsel students and parents on goals, objectives, and plans.
- Rapidly develop and adjust lesson plans to meet unforeseen classroom situations.

- Significantly increased enrollment and student learning by implementing innovative programs.
- Instrumental in state accreditation.